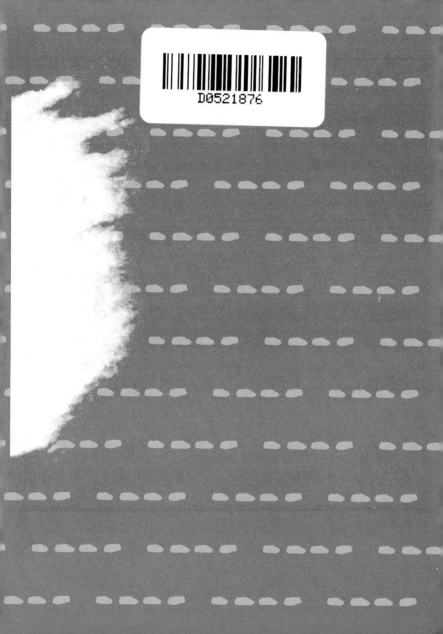

IRiSHiSMS

IRISHISMS

BLATHER, BLARNEY, BLESSINGS AND EVERYTHING ELSE WE SAY IN IRELAND

~~~

RONAN MOORE

GILL BOOKS

GiLL BOOKS
HUME AVENUE
PARK WEST
DUBLiN 12

Gill Books is an imprint of M.H. Gill & Co.

© Ronan Moore 2017

978 07171 7551 2

Edited by Sheila Armstrong
Designed by Fidelma Slattery
Illustrations by Fuchsia MacAree
Printed in Poland by B Z Graf

This book is typeset in Daft Brush and Gotham.

The paper used in this book comes from the wood pulp of managed forests. For every tree felled, at least one tree is planted, thereby renewing natural resources.

A CIP catalogue record for this book is available from the British Library.

5 4 3 2 1

For little Broc

CONTENTS

THE ART OF CONVERSATION

—

The Irish are great talkers who revel in conversation. We love to talk, chat and gossip until the cows come home. Even when they do come home that often leads to more conversations asking the cows how they got on and if there was there any craic. As a result, it is important to know some useful phrases for greeting someone, as well as starting, continuing and ending conversations.

GREETiNGS

Like everyone else in the world, Irish people like to greet each other when they meet. This can change based on location, age, sobriety and whether or not the person owes you money. One common thread between them all is that aside from the 'hello', 'hi' and 'hey', most Irish greetings are questions.

AON SCÉAL? Literally meaning 'any story?', this greeting is popular in and around areas of Ireland where Irish is the lingua franca as well as amongst young men on their way to football training.

WHAT'S THE CRAIC? How are you doing? One of the most common greetings that can be used morning, noon or night.

ANY CRAIC? As above but more commonly employed when the person being asked was out in the pub the previous evening.

ANY SCANDAL? The big different between 'any craic?' and 'any scandal?' is that the person asking wants to hear who you hooked up with and whether you got the shift.

WHAT ABOUT YOU, HI! This is a proper Ulster greeting that can sometimes frighten tourists, particularly those in Derry who are already on edge, unsure if they should call the place Derry, Londonderry or City of Derry! The greeting first begins as a question that makes absolutely no sense – 'what about you'. Then, before the unsuspecting visitor can even begin to guess what is being asked of them, a great big 'HI!' is thrown in at the end to scare the sh*t out of them.

ALRIGHT THERE! Another friendly hello used by our Northern friends who love to add that bit of drama to their greetings.

ALRIGHT? A grittier, no-nonsense form of hello occasionally associated with people wearing hoodies in Dublin city.

STORY? Related to 'Alright?' but a little more social. Thought to have originated from the same guys who brought you horses loose on the M50.

ALRIGHT/STORY BUD? Having the 'bud' at the end means that you have established street cred with the person asking it. If this were a movie, they wouldn't even suspect you of wearing a wire.

WELL JIM? The nice thing about this is that the person being greeted doesn't have to be called Jim, know a Jim or look anything like a Jim.

HOW'S SHE CUTTIN'? If someone local is greeting you like this, well then, as they might say in *The Wizard of Oz*, 'you're a long way from Tallaght, Toto'. This is a country greeting rarely heard in cities outside Croke Park Sundays, Coppers and December 8th shopping sprees.

HOW'S THE FORM? Unless you are asked this in a bookmakers in the middle of Cheltenham, you are being asked about your health. Keep your answer simple.

HOW'S ABOUT YE? This is the same question as above, except you're probably being asked it 100 miles further north.

HOW'S IT GOING? While this greeting allows you to give a more descriptive response, still keep it to one sentence. I mean, you haven't even gotten on to talking about the weather yet!

HOW'S IT HANGING? This is one of those greetings that under absolutely no circumstances should you give a literal reply, i.e. 'slightly too far to the left but the doctor says that's normal as you get older'. Instead, 'Grand', or 'Not a bother', will suffice.

HOWIYA? They managed to put their question into just one word. So you can do the same with your answer.

SURE I'M GRAND

Perhaps the most common way to respond to any question asking after your health is to say that you're average. And our favourite way to say this is with the word 'grand'.

Grand, according to the *Collins English Dictionary*:

Grand/
adjective

1.

magnificent and imposing in appearance, size, or style. 'a grand country house'
synonyms: magnificent, imposing, impressive, awe-inspiring, splendid, resplendent, superb, striking, monumental, majestic, glorious.

2.

denoting the largest or most important item of its kind. 'the grand entrance'
synonyms: main, principal, foremost, major, central, prime.

According to the Irishisms dictionary:

Grand/
adjective

1.
mediocre
'I'm grand'
synonyms: average, ordinary, run-of-the-mill, unexceptional.

Irish people love to say how okay everything is and have a surprising amount of words that do just that. Of all these words, perhaps our most-loved example of this is the word 'grand'.

It is important for visitors to Ireland to note that the Irish 'grand' is as far removed from the English dictionary definition as you can get. It does not mean impressive, majestic or imposing, as in, 'that is a grand castle'. Instead, it means fine, average, mediocre. In fact, grand is the king of 'okays', with a usage as multifunctional as it is mundane. And it is for this reason that perhaps the most popular response to that most basic of questions, 'how are you getting on/how are you doing/how are you feeling?' is the one-word answer: 'Grand'.

So great is the word 'grand' that it can be used in a whole host of other situations.

- Q. 'Would you like tea?' A. 'Thanks, but I'm grand.' = Thanks, but I am okay.

- Q. 'Do you need anything from the shops?' A. 'No, I'm grand.' = No, I don't.

- Q. 'What would you like for dinner?' A. 'Anything at all, I'll be grand with.' = Whatever you are having yourself.

- Q. 'Steak then?' A. 'Grand.' = Sounds good.

- Q. 'I'm heading out later to Marcie's for a quick one.' A. 'That's grand. I'll join you after.' = Perfect, I'll join you after.

OTHER WAYS OF TELLING PEOPLE HOW AVERAGE WE ARE

There are indeed many other ways of saying how average we are feeling other than grand. While all the following are acceptable responses to how you might be feeling, there are certain slightly specific circumstances when you might use one over the other.

DIVIL A BOTHER: A common catch-all rural 'okay' which is used irrespective of whether you have just won the lottery or are on your way home from a funeral.

TIPPING ALONG: You could be on death row or in your second year at college. Tipping along is a wonderful term that basically means you are keeping well, taking each day as it comes.

SWINGING THE DIVIL BY THE TAIL: This tends to be a little bit more positive than its compatriots and can be commonly heard from those over 70 who have decided to take the handbrake off and are now enjoying living life to the full.

KEEPING MOVING: This final grim response is often employed when things aren't going fantastically well – possibly because your girlfriend broke up with you last month; you've just been laid off; or, worse again, your football team were beaten at home by their bitter rivals. 'Keeping moving' gives the impression that if you didn't you'd probably keel over and die.

MIDDLIN': You're not sick but nor are you feeling a million dollars. A good mid-week response.

FINE: While fine should suggest okay, quite often it is a little less than grand. If it comes from your better half, then it is a lot less than grand and you're soon going to know all about it. Trust me, it is not f**kin' fine!

WAYS OF TELLING PEOPLE HOW AVERAGE EVERYTHING ELSE IS

Not content with a half dozen words that are commonly used to tell everyone how okay we are, we also have another half dozen that help people understand how everything else is okay too. While the following phrases could also be employed to describe your state, they usually sound a little better explaining something else.

A-OKAY: In case they didn't hear the 'A' bit, you follow up with 'okay'. You might hear this from players who've just clashed in a contact sport as they persuade their physio that they are fine to continue. 'I'm A-okay' they tell them, even if they aren't totally sure what sport they are meant to be playing. Thankfully, this is now frowned on in the modern game.

A1: Anyone familiar with the old Leaving Certificate would know that an A1 was the best possible grade you could get, equivalent to 100 points and a hell of a lot of hard work. A1 in conversation, on the other hand, does not refer to 100%, but instead means okay. 'I need you to come in a half hour earlier to cover me, is that okay?' 'A1'. 'Our flight is at 4 so we'll need to be leaving here by lunch.' 'A1'. 'Could you drop me into town to meet my friend?' 'A1'.

100%: Again, much like A1, this does not mean something amazing or a top result but merely that you agree with something or think that it's fine. 'We're going to stop in the Foggy Dew on the way for a quick one if that's okay?' '100%'. 'Are you sure you don't mind feeding the dog while I'm away?' 'Don't worry, 100%.' Or even 'I think we should start seeing other people, how does that make you feel?' '100%'.

CÚLA BÚLA: Though this is used to suggest that you are fine with something, 'cúla búla' can also be employed when you're acting like a sociopathic member of a television crime gang.

NO WORRIES: This is perhaps the closest to the 'okay' we use when something is not okay, like when a work colleague used up the last of your peanut butter, when yer wan cancels a date at the last minute, or when a mother of three is apologising after her little Luke threw up over you at the check-out counter. 'No worries' you tell them all.

NOT A BOTHER: This 'okay' is a lot more positive and increases in popularity towards the weekend. It is a favourite response of people during the honeymoon stage of their new relationship/car/job. 'How's it going?' 'Not a bother.' Give them time.

SOUND: Once again, not to be mixed up with the dictionary definition, as in 'vibrations that travel through the air or another medium and which can be heard when they reach a person's ear', but sound as in 'grand'. While 'sound' is nearly as multifunctional as 'grand', it can sometimes be used to imply a more positive form of okay, especially when referring to that referee/manager/teacher that most other people think is a bollix, e.g. 'Ah no, I think he's sound.' If you really want to reinforce the positivity, because he lent you a tenner, didn't send you off or gave you a good mark in your essay, you can say 'dead sound'.

SOUND AS A TROUT: An idiom so elegant it is a wonder why everyone in the country doesn't use this western phrase.

THE WEATHER

Having greeted each other and given some level of response, it is important to remember that before most Irish people will engage in any sort of decent conversation they first have to visit the two mainstays of Irish conversations – the weather and who you both have in common.*
While there is not much to finding out who you have in common, it can certainly prove helpful to understand some key terminology when it comes to the weather.

*WHO YOU BOTH HAVE IN COMMON: As well as the weather, Irish people never truly feel comfortable talking to strangers, specifically those with some level of connection to Ireland, until they discover who you both have in common. This could be that they were served a sandwich once in Boston by a woman whose sister was the babysitter of your cousin's class-mate. That will suffice and thus allow conversation to take place.

༄ **... we're having:** This is perhaps the most important part of a sentence when talking about the weather and knowing this will safely put you on the front foot in any weather-related conversations. To make it work, simply add some description of weather in front of it and the

person spoken to will agree, i.e. 'Great weather ... we're having.' 'Terrible weather ... we're having.' 'Wet weather ... we're having.' 'Savage weather ... we're having.' 'Mighty weather ... we're having.' 'Awful weather ... we're having.' 'Weather weather ... we're having.'

While the description may have little in common with the actual weather is immaterial. It is more important to simply comment on the weather than to actually tie it to reality.

- **A grand stretch in the evenings:** While this can be used any time from December 21st, it comes into its own around the beginning of February when whole villages can be heard conversing about it.

- **Sunny spells and scattered showers:** Our weather for 95% of the year.

- **Promising:** Another key word in our weather dictionary is 'promising'. Despite having weather that has all the predictability of a schizophrenic frog, Irish people love to state how the weathermen promised them something. It might be lashing rain outside but the weatherman 'promised' it will turn sunny later. Snowing now, but he 'promised it would turn a lot milder by the weekend'. Nothing but greyness overhead the last fortnight, but 'promising to brighten up by this evening'.

- **You won't see winter coming:** While this might be used any time from June 21st, its usage kicks off the first day you can't get away with wearing a T-shirt, which to Irish people is generally below 12°C.

- **Roasting:** Five days of prolonged sunshine with daytime temperatures over 20°C.

- **A scorcher:** A day of prolonged sunshine with daytime temperatures over 25°C.

- **Bucketing down:** Severe rainfall. The type of rain where you are not sure if you should make a run for the door or stay in the car until it passes. Tip: Stay in the car until it passes.

- **Pissing:** Sounds a little offensive, and would probably not go down well on TV if you were to say that it's 'pissing down for today's All-Ireland Final'. However, we all know it simply means raining heavily and steadily.

- **Lashing:** Perhaps our favourite type of rain of the 453 varieties we have in this country. Not as heavy as when it's bucketing down, but certainly more than when it's pissing.

- **Nippy:** No need to over-react, but if you feel the evenings getting nippy you might need to re-order the oil for the winter.

- **Bitter:** Really cold, like nearly freezing!

- **Skin ya alive:** This term is particularly useful for when you're describing an east wind that would 'skin ya alive!'

HOW THE WEATHER IS MAKING YOU FEEL

If you are going to spend so much time talking about the weather, it is no harm to also be able to talk about how the weather is making you feel.

~ **Frozen:** No, I don't want to build a f**kin snowman! I want to be inside beside a fire. Speaks for itself really.

~ **Foundered:** This is to be absolutely frozen up north.

~ **Famished:** This is to be absolutely frozen down south (though if someone says this in July it means they're starving).

~ **Perished:** What happens to you when you lock yourself out and are waiting for the house-mate to come home and let you back in.

~ **Drownded:** We know we could spell it drowned, but we choose not to because that's not how wet we actually are – 'we're effin drownded!'

~ **Meltin':** What you feel like when it gets into the 20s and you've got your jeans on.

CONVERSATION

When you have completed the formalities, proper conversation can begin. In Ireland, there is a variety of conversations we enjoy being engaged in.

CHIN-WAG: Traditionally done over the garden fence, this type of talk is just as common at the water-cooler or while collecting children. A chin-wag stays on the right side of positive and doesn't involve rumours and hearsay.

GOSSIP: Involves nothing but rumours and hearsay.

BITCH AND A MOAN: This is obviously on the other side of positive and when you need to just vent about your idiot colleague at work, the boss who is giving you stick, the children that are driving you up the wall or the husband who won't bring his own f**in' mug to the sink when he's finished his tea!

CHIT-CHAT: This is conversation that covers everything and anything, and which can take place everywhere from the check-out counter to the doctor's waiting room. It is casual, calm and relaxed, unless it hits upon a serious topic and becomes a 'heart-to-heart'.

HEART-TO-HEART: A heart-to-heart is the type of low-voiced conversation that deals with issues of great importance like the home life, the ill health and the 'you know yourself'. Tissues are sometimes used, as are a pint/mug of tea and frequent hugs. We men don't do enough of it in Ireland – well, not until Bressie came on the scene.

BANTER: This is the chat and laughter best had early on a Friday evening, when the whole weekend is ahead of you and you are catching up with pals over a few nice pints.

BANTS: Every bit as much fun as banter, but just that little bit younger.

CRAIC: We'll talk more about craic later, but essentially craic is that type of conversation where only things of light humour are spoken about – so no politics, no long-term relationships and no religion.

CONVERSATION FILLERS

It is important not to put yourself under too much pressure in conversation, particularly amongst large groups. Indeed, visitors to Ireland can struggle in Irish conversations, sometimes because they do not know what to say and other times because they don't know what is being said! Here are a selection of conversation fillers that can be used almost indiscriminately during a chat to help you along. They can be split roughly into two blocks.

Those that kind of make sense:

- **I know, I know, I know:** Whether you know or not, this makes it sound like you care about what is being said.

- **It is what it is:** Doesn't matter if you don't know what 'is' was in the first place, this is perfect for just saying 'that's that'.

- **Ah stop:** While sometimes you genuinely wish they would, 'ah stop' is a nice vanilla-flavoured filler for any chat.

- **Where would you be going?** This response is tailor-made for when a person tells you about a great deal they got down at their local Penneys/Lidl/SuperValu/family-owned menswear store.

- **Don't get me started:** When you agree (or pretend to agree) with the speaker's anger over a certain subject.

- **Ah sure, you'll get that:** Like the above, and perfect for when the speaker sounds exasperated by a certain topic.

- **Small towns and built-up areas:** 'Ah sure, you'll get that', except more for the urban area.

- **Chickens today, feathers tomorrow:** 'Ah sure, you'll get that' except more for the rural area. Neither 'small towns' nor 'chickens' should be used when the person is talking about a matter of some gravity. I mean, on the occasion of a death in the family, no one will draw comfort from you telling them 'chickens today, feathers tomorrow'!

- **Exactly!:** A nice reinforcement for a concluding point, but if you don't know what they are talking about, this should be avoided, as such certainty on your part when announcing 'exactly' often leads them to asking 'so, what do you think?'

Those that kind of don't make sense:

- **You know yourself:** Either we're telling them that they are aware of what they are talking about, throwing out a deep metaphysical statement or we're just filling the conversation.

- **Are sure look!:** Look at what? There's nothing to look at! But that doesn't stop us telling you to anyway!

- **Sure listen!:** Well, they are listening, it's called a conversation so we don't need to remind you! It doesn't stop us, however.

- **Would ye stop?:** Stop what? Listening? Nodding your head in agreement? Replying with occasional nods of affirmation? In fact, nothing, we want you to stop nothing!

- **Come here to me:** Don't, you're near enough. It's just something we say to keep you listening.

- **Like:** Originating somewhere in Dublin before spreading nationwide, 'like' is oft put at the end, middle or beginning of a sentence like. Absolutely no comparison is being made. In certain parts of the capital it is pronounced 'loike', as in 'loike, I really loike a few scoops, loike.'

CONVERSATION ENDERS

There comes a time when every conversation must come to an end. Bringing it to a conclusion is not always easy, especially when you're stuck talking to someone you don't like. Having greeted them, mentioned the weather and then pretended to listen for just the right amount of time so as not to appear like a right bollix, choose from one of the following phrases to help bring the conversation to a close.

... **Sure, that's it so:** You have exhausted all conversation and to hang around any longer would just be embarrassing for the both of ye.

... **Right so:** A friendly way to finish, which suggests you've got your fill of good company and conversation.

... **Look, I best be off:** You can add some second sentence that mumbles off into nothingness but doing so might force them out of politeness to ask you 'what is it that you best be off to?' Instead, just look at your watch, whether you have one or not, and leave with a bye.

... I better let you go/I better not keep you: Though this is perfect for phone conversations that need to wind up, it can also be used in person. Of course, these two responses always work better in phone calls and conversations that you initiated. Don't worry, by the time they realised that it was them who rang or stopped you, you'll be long gone.

... Anyways: This is a brave one, but pays off if you can stomach the silence that inevitably follows it – 'Anyways ...' If you can stop yourself from filling in the blank, then just stand up, take your coat and leave. If you think that ending is too *Wolf of Wall Street*, then you can always throw in a 'I best be off' as you are putting on your coat.

... Sin é: Literally meaning 'that's it' as Gaeilge – uttering this as you rise, stretch and look out the window will bring any conversation to a satisfactory conclusion even if they haven't got around to telling you whether their wife has actually left them or not.

GOODBYES

While there are as many ways to say goodbye as there are elsewhere in the English-speaking world, we do have a few that are that little bit more uniquely Irish.

SLÁN: Perhaps the easiest piece of Irish you can learn and use in common conversation. Slán always works well with a wave, even if you are on the phone.

SEE YA LATER: Perhaps the most popular form of goodbye you'll hear in Ireland.

BYE, BYE, BYE: is a popular way to finish a phone conversation, though it can confuse the person on the other end who may think they are picking up some feedback.

CHAT TO YA: I have to go now but I have more to tell you later about what she got up to last night.

TALK TO YOU SOON: Common farewell irrespective of whether they are taking off for Mount Everest or heading to bed.

GOOD LUCK: This goodbye is a national favourite and one that has left many a workmate Down Under scratching their head. 'Good luck' with what? Getting home safely? Switching off? Eating dinner in front of the TV?

TAKE IT EASY: Good luck and don't be fretting about storm warnings, deadlines or Donald Trump.

CAREFUL NOW/PLAY IT SAFE/SAFE TRAVEL/MIND HOW YOU GO: This is for those leaving and driving home. Basically, the well-wisher is telling you to wear your seat belt, pull over if you feel tired, slow down when the lights turn amber and if you are visiting from abroad not to forget to drive on the left.

ALL THE BEST: It was a great night, see you soon and I hope you win the lottery or at the very least are not hungover in the morning.

A final note of interest is that it is totally fine, particularly amongst close friends, to add a term of abuse at the end, such as 'see ya later, ya ol' bollix' or 'chat ya again, you miserable shite'. Don't try this if it is the first time you have met the person or on any occasion you are with your father-in-law, no matter how well you think you may know him.

WHERE WE'RE FROM

—

Before we get too far ahead of ourselves it might be good to reflect on where all these greetings, words and phrases are used – Ireland.

IRELAND: WHAT'S IN A NAME?

While how we refer to our home might come as second nature to those of us living here, for those coming from abroad it can sometimes be terribly confusing.

Ireland: This is our official name and the default option for what we should be called. 'This', of course, being the twenty-six counties that are predominantly southern in nature. As for the other six ... we'll have to come back to them later.

The Republic of Ireland: This is not our official name, though few people will correct you if you use it. While we are a republic, we don't officially call ourselves this. I mean, if our country had a driving licence it would say 'Ireland' and not 'the Republic of Ireland' on it, in the same way a driving licence says 'Joe Bloggs' and not 'the Human of Joe Bloggs'. Only organisations like FIFA and our friends in the United Kingdom refer to us as the Republic of Ireland. That is why when they invite us over for a birthday party they usually start with 'Dear Republic of Ireland, would you like to …' to which we usually respond, 'we'd love to come, yours truly, Ireland'.

Éire: The Irish spelling of Ireland is derived from the Gaelic goddess Eriú. Due to its four-letter length, Éire is a popular tattoo, particularly amongst die-hard football fans who realise that having a 'Republic of Ireland' tattoo just doesn't have the same ring to it. We don't tend to use Éire in conversation.

Northern Ireland: Booooooooooo! Northern Ireland is the pantomime villain of Irish geography classes. It represents the six counties under the _____ * of the United Kingdom. While these six counties have _____* long periods of devolved government under the name of the Northern Ireland Assembly, by and large people living down south in Ireland generally don't use the term Northern Ireland. As a visitor, no one will give out to you for using it, just don't be super enthusiastic when you do.

The North: It can be easy to see why tourists sometimes get mixed up between the North in Ireland and the North in George R. R. Martin's series of books. After all, a lot of *Game of Thrones* is filmed here, both places have experienced bloody battles over territory, contain different communities wishing to practise their own traditions in

• Fill in the blanks as necessary.

peace, and let's not forget that whole Orange Marcher/White Walker thing. That being said, Ireland's North and Westeros' North are both very different. I mean, have you ever heard a Wildling say 'HI!?' at the end of a sentence? 'You know nothing, Jon Snow, HI!?' One clear connection though is the name, 'the North', which is a perfectly acceptable term when referring to Northern Ireland.

The Island of Ireland: A very diplomatic term for both parts of the island. However, unless you have been asked to open an Apple Festival in Armagh or an Arts Week in Coleraine, there is probably no reason to find yourself employing this term in everyday chat.

The Six Counties: If someone says this to you they are probably not a fan of the six counties being kept apart from the other twenty-six counties. I would discourage responses such as 'you mean Northern Ireland, don't you?'

Erin's Isle: This is the most popular poetic name for the island of Ireland. While we never use this unless we are writing poetry, it might cause a few Irish eyes in Chicago and Boston to go misty if they hear it, such is the romantic imagery the name conjures up.

Eireann/Eirinn: Both refer to Ireland but we don't use these as a stand-alone title. The reason for this is due to the fact that they are genitive nouns (or dative nouns or some other nouns they didn't teach us about in primary school because we were too busy tracing chestnut leaves into our nature copy).

The Green Isle: Unless you are referring to Ireland's largest frozen food producer, don't use this one.

Hibernia: Unfortunately this has fallen out of general usage since its heyday when every Roman worth his salt referred to us as Hibernia. Of course, they, like Strabo, a geographer living under Julius Caesar's rule, also liked to refer to us as 'a cannibal race who deemed it commendable to devour [our] deceased fathers.' Good times.

THE COUNTY YOU HAIL FROM

Though Ireland is a relatively small place, people are very fond of the specific location they come from. While this can break down all the way to the house, the street, the parish or the village you grew up in, at a basic level it comes down to which county you call home. Divided by rivers, lakes, mountains or diesel-laundering plants, each of these 32 counties has at least one nickname that the visitor (especially a visitor who is expecting to marry someone from the county) should know. To help you remember what's what, we have split the counties into a number of categories.

NICKNAMES RELATED TO PEOPLE OR FAMILIES WHO ONCE LIVED THERE:

DONEGAL: 'The Tir Conaill Men', related to the medieval kingdom that gave the county its name.

WATERFORD: 'The Deise', referring to the medieval kingdom of the Déisi.

LAOIS: 'O'More County', indicating the medieval family most associated with Laois.

MONAGHAN: 'Farney County', due to the medieval territory of Farney.

CAVAN: 'Breffni County', signifying the medieval kingdom of Breifne.

TYRONE: 'The Red Hand County', which is down to the crest of the medieval O'Neill's who controlled this part of the country.

GALWAY: 'The Tribesmen', representing the fourteen medieval families who used to control the city.

SLIGO: 'Yeats Country', denoting no medieval kingdom but instead the great Irish poet and occasional bugbear of Leaving Cert students, W. B. Yeats.

LONGFORD: 'The Slashers', not suggesting those who get off a stag party bus for a quick wee, but Myles 'the Slasher' O'Reilly, who was killed as he bravely defended the bridge of Finnea in 1644.

NICKNAMES RELATED TO THE COLOUR OF THE COUNTY JERSEYS:

ANTRIM: 'The Saffrons', which won out over 'the Browny Oranges', 'the Mustards' and 'the Donald Trumps'.

KILDARE: 'The Lilywhites', due to their whiteness, which isn't a race thing – honest.

NICKNAMES RELATED TO NATURAL AND GEOGRAPHICAL FEATURES:

LEITRIM: 'The Ridge County', denoting Leitrim's beautiful ridges in the northwest.

ARMAGH: 'The Orchard County', due to the bountiful cider-producing apple orchards.

WICKLOW: 'The Garden County', not only because of its wonderful gardens, but because of the exquisite natural beauty.

FERMANAGH: 'The Ernesiders', representing the stunning river Erne.

WESTMEATH: 'The Lake County', referring to the many lakes of Westmeath.

DOWN: 'The Mournemen', describing the mysterious Mourne Mountains.

DERRY: 'The Oak Leaf', due to the … er … wonderful oak leaves.

NICKNAMES RELATED TO SIZE OR LOCATION:

MAYO: 'The Westerners', because that's where they are.

LOUTH: 'The Wee County', because it's not very big.

NICKNAMES RELATED TO SOMEWHAT UNFORTUNATE SOUNDING PAST HABITS:

CARLOW: 'The Scallion-eaters', because they once sold them.

ROSCOMMON: 'The Sheep-stealers', because they once stole them.

NICKNAMES RELATED TO HISTORICAL EVENTS:

LIMERICK: 'The Treaty County', derived from the 1691 Treaty of Limerick.

CLARE: 'The Banner County', thought to come from Daniel O'Connell's banner of Catholic Emancipation.

OFFALY: 'The Faithful County', surprisingly not reflecting some loyalty to king, queen or leader, but rather because some guy called Andy Croke called it this way back in 1953!

NICKNAMES RELATED TO HISTORICAL EVENTS THAT ALSO SOUND GREAT:

WEXFORD: 'The Model County', not due to Enniscorthy once rivalling the fashion capitals of London, Paris and Milan, but rather the county's long tradition of model farming methods.

MEATH: 'The Royal County', where the High Kings of Ireland were seated.

KERRY: 'The Kingdom', which it was derogatively referred to all the way back in 1787 by John Curran, when he suggested that it may as well have been a different country from England – something I'm sure the locals continue to happily accept.

CORK: 'The Rebels', because of their support for the pretender Perkin Warbeck, their role in the War of Independence and because they just don't give a damn what anyone thinks about them.

KILKENNY: 'The Cats', which is not because of the number of stray tabbies that can be found in and around Kilkenny city, but supposedly due to English soldiers tying two together during the Cromwellian war to see them fight.

NICKNAMES THAT JUST MAKE THE COUNTY SOUND GREAT:

TIPPERARY: 'The Premier County', thought to be due to its wonderfully fertile land.

AND THEN, FINALLY, NICKNAMES THAT ARE NOT REALLY IMAGINATIVE BUT ARE MEMORABLE ALL THE SAME:

DUBLIN: 'The Dubs', because Dub is short for Dublin.

OTHER PLACES PEOPLE HAIL FROM

Aside from counties there are other places people might occasionally tell you where they or you hail from.

The Pale: Originating from the French word *pālus*, meaning stake, the Pale was the English-controlled area of Dublin and surrounding areas. Nowadays it is pretty much anywhere with an area code beginning with 'D'.

The Big Smoke: Referring to the city proper of Dublin and not its strawberry-growing commuter belts.

D4: The Beverly Hills 90210 of Dublin, with fewer palm trees and more fake tan.

The Long Grass: Outside of Dublin.

The Wesht: Anywhere west of the Shannon.

The People's Republic: This does not have to be completed for you to know that the person is referring to Cork. If they say 'boy' at the end of it, then they are actually *from* the People's Republic.

THE PERSON
YOU ARE

Finally, just in case there is any lingering confusion as to where you come from, a further category of identifiers can be employed to sort out who you are based on where you're from.

- **Jackeen:** Someone from Dublin, so-called because of their pre-independence disposition to hanging the Union Jack out their windows for British royal visits. But at least they had windows!

- **Culchie:** A term used mostly by people from Dublin for those living in the countryside – with the countryside being any village and most urban centres outside of the capital.

- **Buffer:** Someone who is living in the commuter belt between Dublin and the rest of the country.

- **Bogger:** Used by urban dwellers across Ireland for those living deep in the countryside. 'Deep in the countryside' generally signifies that they live on a farm, have access to a tractor and are or were a member of Macra na Feirme.

- **Muck savage:** The country cousin of a bogger. To the uneducated eye, a 'muck-savage' is someone from the back-end of the arse-end of nowhere who can be seen outside Supermacs swearing loudly with a mouthful of chips on their way up to Croker on a championship Sunday. To the educated eye, it is someone with feelings and fears and dreams and desires and a mouthful of chips swearing loudly on their way up to Croker on a championship Sunday.

- **From down the country:** Just to completely cut itself off from everywhere else in Ireland, this is a term used exclusively by Dublin dwellers for those living in the countryside – basically the rest of Ireland outside the M50 (the ring road that surrounds the capital).

- **Blow-in:** A term employed for someone not originally from the area. By and large, it doesn't matter if you have lived somewhere for 50 years, do the church collections, run a pub, score the winning point in the village's first county championship final, marry the daughter of yer man or save a dozen young children from a burning building. Unless you were born in the village, have a parent buried in the village or at the very least did your Holy Communion in the village then you will always be a blow-in.

- **BIFFO:** A big ignorant fat so-and-so from Offaly. Or, if you are actually from the county, it means a beautiful intelligent female from Offaly.

- **BUFFALO:** A big ignorant fat so-and-so from around Laois and Offaly.

- **Dulchie:** This is a special category of blow-ins used to denote Dublin natives now living in the country.

DOWN THE COUNTRY

Though Ireland is increasingly becoming an urbanised nation, we still are drawn back to the countryside, with many, many Irish people only a generation or two out of the fields. Consequently, whether you are from the big city or from abroad, it is no harm to know a few terms about this place.

Boreen: The small roads that pock-mark the length and breadth of the countryside and are characterised by grass verges that run up their centre. Kind, elderly uncles usually live up them.

Cattle grids: Defence mechanism at the front gates of country homes designed to keep out cattle and people using crutches.

Ditch: The line of hedgerow that runs along most country roads and where most cars end up if they are driving too fast on a frosty morning. Also the place your mother assumes you're dead in if you don't ring her every day.

Silage: This is the somewhat fermented stored fodder that farmers give to their livestock, particularly during the winter months. It can sometimes smell.

Slurry: This is the somewhat fermented animal waste and whatever you're having yourself that collects in pits and which farmers spread over the fields in the dry months. It can really smell.

Slurry pit: Think hippopotamuses and crocs in the Zambezi, box jellyfish off the Sydney coast, Great Whites in the water near the Cape – would you go near these? No. Then never, ever go near a slurry pit. Most dangerous square footage in Ireland.

Yard: The main square of the farm. The only place where visiting townie cousins are told they are allowed to play and even then, be careful if you hear a tractor coming, that'll be your uncle driving in for lunch.

There are also a few mythical characteristics of the country that it can do no harm to understand.

Fairy fort: If you ever come across a raised, roundish piece of untouched land surrounded by bushes in the middle of a ploughed field, it could in all likelihood be a fairy fort. These circular mounds, often derived from more ancient embankments, are still considered sacred. Almost every farming family knows at least one story of someone who dug into a fairy fort with his JCB, became cursed and died peacefully in his sleep some 50 years later!

Stray sod: Effectively a mythological landmine in a field. When stood on, this will immediately disorientate the rambler. They will quickly become lost and not know where they are until they are discovered by a passer-by several hours later or just sober up and leave via the gate they came in.

PLACES WE BE AT

When defining where someone is at a given moment Irish people have a tendency to be quite descriptive. Rather than say 'John is in Dublin' or 'Helen is at the shops', we like to use every preposition going.

OVER: e.g. He is 'over' in Athlone for the weekend.

DOWN: e.g. She has got the train 'down' to Cork.

ACROSS: e.g. She's gone 'across' to Galway to meet himself.

BELOW: e.g. She is studying 'below' in Waterford.

UP: e.g. He went 'up' to Belfast for New Years.

AROUND: e.g. He's stays 'around' Dublin during the week.

AWAY: e.g. She's 'away' at college in Sligo.

ADIN: inside, e.g. He's 'adin' in the house watching the TV.

ADOUT: outside, e.g. We was 'adout' down the fields rounding up the cattle.

A word of caution, however, in that sometimes the location the person might be referring to could be less physical and more metaphysical.

— If you heard that Malachy was **'up a tree in Rosemount'** what they actually mean is that no one has a clue where Malachy is.

— And if someone told you that Michael was **'circling over Shannon'** they wouldn't mean you'd find him 12,000 feet in the air – instead he'd be propping up the bar drunk in Fitzgerald's down the road. 'Circling over Shannon' is thought to have come from the time Russian Premier Boris Yeltsin was so 'sick'* he was unable to get off his official plane in Shannon.

*scuttered drunk.

HOME
AND
FAMILY

—

Family and the home are very important in Ireland, and while we no longer have as many double-digit family units as we once had, parents, siblings and wider relations still make up 75% of the people we invite to our weddings.

PARENTS

With the height of respect for our parents, the Irish have a wide range of terms to describe the wonderful pair who brought us into this world.

- **Da folks:** The type of parents you don't mind pulling up outside your house unannounced on a Sunday afternoon, as in, 'Who's that just pulling in?' 'Oh, it's just da folks'. 'Oh great, I'll just throw on the kettle so.'

- **Da ol' pair:** The type of parents you do mind pulling up outside your house unannounced on a Sunday afternoon, as in, 'Who's that just pulling in?' 'Oh feck, it's da ol' pair, draw the curtains there quick!'

- **Ma:** As in 'me Ma', who I love to bits.

- **Da:** As in 'me Da', who I love to bits, though I wish he wouldn't keep climbing onto the roof to fix the television aerial and him nearly 80.

- **The ol' lad:** Your father when he has retired and spends most of his time either golfing, doing Sudoku or fixing the neighbour's broken microwaves.

- **Memmeh:** This is what a country mother becomes when you move to the city. Memmehs can be divided into 'phone

Memmeh', who rings you up every Wednesday to see when you're coming home, and 'techie Memmeh'. 'Techie Memmeh' also wants to know when you're home but can send you WhatsApp messages with pictures of the cat.

> **Deddeh:** Married to Memmeh and is the person who usually answers the phone and asks how the weather is in Dublin before passing you over to Memmeh – unless, of course, someone has died, in which case they'll tell you all about this first.

> **Doll:** Donegal term for a woman, a wife or a mother.

> **Aul boy:** Your Dad, especially in the north-west.

> **Dad, Daddy, Mam, Mammy:** Other self-explanatory terms that we tend to use.

And then there are words we do not use for our parents:

> **Mummy:** Only employed when you are twenty-four going on five, are afraid of the dark and love Enid Blyton.

> **Mummsy:** Only used by those who inherited a 1,000-hectare estate complete with game, manor house and stables.

> **Papa:** Not unless you are a Smurf.

> **Pop:** Not uttered unless you have recently moved to Ireland from the American Mid-West.

CHILDREN

Irish children also hold a special place in our nation's heart, particularly those that are not teenagers. To reflect this there is a lengthy list of terms of endearment that parents, aunts, uncles, godparents and grandparents use.

- **Gossin:** A 'gossin' is a young boy that is generally very pleasant and can be trusted to look after his younger sister. Often referred to as 'a grand young gossin', they tend to clear up during Communions.

- **Me ol' segotia:** While it is not unusual for one 70 year-old retiree at the bar to welcome in another 70-year-old retiree with 'me ol' segotia', strangely enough this is just as commonly used for young girls, particularly those who bring their grandfathers over their slippers.

- **Skutcher:** Another fond term that can be used for both boys and girls, primarily those under the age of five who don't talk back at you.

- **Scut:** Same as above, but for children between the ages of five and eight.

✏ **Babby:** This is how several of your aunts will refer to little Saoirse, asking 'how's the babby?', even if little Saoirse is a long way from being a 'babby' anymore. You can respond with any of the following: 'she's almost walking', 'out of nappies' or 'started college last September'.

✏ **Snapper:** Made eternally famous by the film of the same name, 'snapper' means a little kid that does not have to be the progeny of Georgie Burgess.

✏ **Whippersnapper:** Also meaning a little kid, although one who is more likely to jump from table to couch before they reach the age of two.

✏ **Wee one:** Little child, especially up north.

✏ **Wean:** Another north-western name for a child just a little older than the 'wee one'.

✏ **Canat:** Old-timey expression for a little girl who looks mischievous even if she has yet to be caught tying your shoelaces together or pouring milk on the floor for the cat.

✏ **Childer:** What some call their children down the country, and is used when you're in front of the judge: 'please your 'onour, don't send me and the childer to the poorhouse.'

ൟ **Gartler:** Happy little girl who loves nothing more than to sit on a relative's knee and tell them all about school, rockets, dinosaurs and anything else that pops into her head.

ൟ **Clouster:** Though you can grow up and still be a 'clouster', its best use is when describing a child up north who has just dropped a forkful of food down their top.

ൟ **Avick:** Perhaps not as angelic as 'gossins', 'avicks' are young boys who tend to fall out of trees and come in covered in muck.

ൟ **Dote:** One of the nicest descriptions that you can use for a little girl. 'Dotes' will always smile when they see you, give you a funny wave when you leave, point out random stuff and go 'oh!', help 'empty' the dishwasher, and even when they are responsible for breaking something their mouth-open, eyes-wide expression is so adorable you couldn't even dream of giving out.

ൟ **Chisler:** Everyone loves 'chislers'. They are cheeky, funny and precocious. They are also bold, brazen and impudent and the type of cheeky kid who will use the kitchen table to raft down the local river, dye the dog blue or board an Air India plane to New York unaccompanied.

ൟ **Skallywag:** You know those cute toddlers with the hilarious facial expressions who love to throw sh... stuff on the floor just to see you pick it up? Skallywags. You can also have a real skallywag who will be out the door and halfway up the stairs as you bend down to pick said item up.

- ❧ **Colleen:** Derived from 'cailín', this is how you refer to your niece, 'a lovely colleen', who's just got 8 A's and 2 B's in her Junior Cert, who always helps with the washing up, sets the table on Sunday and is happy to go shopping with her mother and never forgets the paper for her Dad. Her younger brothers hate her!

- ❧ **Skitters:** Not as annoying as the skutters, 'skitters' are irritating children, usually spoilt.

One final thing about children is that no matter what sort of child they are, there is always a chance that they might **'make strange'** when approached.

MAKE STRANGE: This is when a child who is the most happy-go-lucky and outgoing little thing at home suddenly goes all quiet, withdrawn or even hysterical when meeting a person they are not used to. While this can be deeply uncomfortable for the person, as it does feel like the child has mixed you up with some convicted serial killer, it is just the child 'making strange'. Don't worry – even if you're their Dad – they'll get over it.

AFFECTION

When talking about our loved ones, while we pretend to hold everyone in the same level of affection, there are always clear favourites who, as a result, are more likely to inherit the farm. You'll know these people by the following terms.

HAVE GREAT TIME FOR: You can identify when someone 'has great time for' a niece or nephew. They always ask how they are getting on in college, make an effort at every visit to hear how work is going and are interested in the most banal details of their personal life.

SOFT SPOT: On the surface there is little to separate 'having great time for' someone and having a 'soft spot' for someone. The main difference, however, is that the person who is usually the object of the soft spot is more than likely a familial black sheep.

GRÁ: Meaning to have a love of something. While this is more often heard when referring to a subject or skill, like 'she has a real grá for the Maths' or 'he has a real grá for the haberdashery', it is not unheard of to describe someone's fondness for a niece or nephew.

ACTING UP

While 95% of the time children are funny, adorable, wonderful human beings, they can sometimes misbehave. In Ireland, we have several terms that help categorise types of misbehaviour.

Messing: This is the type of behaviour that is all well and good until someone loses an eye or has the television pulled down on top of them.

Only messing: Like messing except even more dangerous.

Play acting: Usually means pretending to be more annoyed/upset/injured than the reality. Important for parents to first look around their crying children for signs of spilt tea, over-turned televisions, hot irons or nettles before they accuse them of play acting.

Carrying on: A distant cousin to messing, and the main reason why children present themselves back indoors with cut knees, snotty noses and tears. Carrying on is usually self-inflicted and the parents will remind the child, 'I warned you not to be carrying on' as they sticky-plaster the cut.

Caffling: The type of messing children got up to long before smart phones, which inevitably ends up with someone falling out of a tree.

Acting the maggot: This is probably the worst type of idiot behaviour someone might be involved in. Not only is it stupid, it is reckless and upsetting your sister.

Fair bold: Also known as **'pure bold'** this was the type of misbehaviour that meant your Mum or Dad would be told of it when they got home from work. If you want some advice, I'd say you'd better get to bed and pretend to be asleep when they do!

THE IRISH HOME

While an Irish home has much of the same characteristics as most homes across the world – kitchen, bedroom, bathroom, tables, chairs, tat – there are a few features that visitors might be a little less familiar with.

— **The press:** Neither the title of a now-defunct national daily newspaper or a wrestling star's signature move, but the word we use for cupboards in Ireland.

— **Hot press:** The king of cupboards, the hot press, used to be where clothes went to get aired. Unfortunately, with the advent of lagging jackets and washer-dryers, they are no longer as common.

— **The front room:** Though the front room was once indeed at the front of the house, it is more synonymous with the most important room, bar none. As a result, the only things that are allowed in there are family photos, crystal won at golf competitions, coffins (during wakes), priests or wealthy American cousins.

— **Leaba:** The bed in Irish, which people often use when they tell you they're 'off to the leaba'.

— **Immersion:** The way we used to heat up the hot water back in the day. Not knowing if they had remembered to turn off the immersion turned many a family car around before the holiday even got going, and them already in Kinnegad! Unfortunately (or fortunately if you are an Irish teenager), immersions have gone the same way as hot presses, CFCs and asbestos roofs.

— **The wooden spoon:** Not *a* wooden spoon but *the* wooden spoon! For generations, it was the enforcer of rules in the Irish house. Now, however, it is a mixing utensil that you can't even put into a dishwasher. Oh, how the mighty have fallen!

— **Gaff:** Another name for someone's home, but one that strangely doesn't have as many of the above features and certainly no front room!

THiNGS YOU MiGHT OVERHEAR iN AN IRiSH HOUSEHOLD

Here are some things Irish mothers can still be heard saying and what these phrases actually mean.

Stop acting the maggot! (Quit messing.)

Cop on, will ya? (Quit messing.)

Will you stop that carry on? (Quit messing.)

Do you want me to get your father to pull over? (This is really your final warning to quit messing.)

Didn't I tell you that was going to happen? (Serves you right.)

I have a few messages to get in town. (I'm off to the shops.)

The cat wants to get out there now. (Let the cat out, will ya?)

What's the puss for? (Why are you looking so sad?)

Tea, anyone? (I am making tea and someone will to have drink it.)

Throw on the kettle, will ya? (Don't throw anything but carefully fill the kettle up and turn it on).

Did someone leave a door open? (You left the door open, close it!)

I have a letter for you here, would you like me to open it? (I have already opened your post – would you like me to read it to you?)

Where do you think you're off gallivanting to? (Dinner is in half an hour so don't be gone long.)

Don't be at yourself. (You're seven and you're scratching yourself where you shouldn't be, stop it!)

Would you not bring a coat with you? (Bring a coat.)

We haven't got all day! (Be quick, I'm waiting!)

Similarly, here are some things Irish fathers can still be heard saying and what these phrases actually mean.

Did you check your car for oil? (Give me your keys because I don't trust you to look after your car.)

Cut out that racket! (You're making too much noise and I can't hear *Mrs Brown's Boys* even though I have it on full blast.)

Is that what you call music? (The sound coming out from that stereo is horrendous.)

I'll put your mother on. (No one has died so I have nothing left to say to you.)

Sure of course that happened to you. (I could see that accident coming.)

What do you have to say for yourself? (I'm stalling until your mother arrives so she can deal with it.)

Finally, we have things Irish children can still be heard saying and what these phrases actually mean.

I was only messing. (I was deliberately messing with the sole purpose of upsetting my sister.)

I was just saying. (I was deliberately saying with the sole purpose of upsetting my sister.)

Are we there yet? (I'm bored.)

Are we there yet? (I'm really bored.)

Are we there yet? (I'm really, really bored.)

Can we stop in a shop on the way home? (I kept my end of the bargain during that visit to the uncles, now can you buy me sweets?)

PEOPLE

—

When it comes to the names, nicknames and types of people in Ireland we are not found wanting. Indeed, there are so many that it can prove helpful to divide people into groups. That way, if you are introduced to the extended family of Seans, Saoirses and Sorchas who are buckos, battle-axes and bleedin' ticks you'll at least know what to expect.

NAMES

While traditional English and international names such as Jack, James and Daniel, along with Emily, Sophie and Ava continue to dominate the lists in Ireland, we are not short of our own native names that fit into a number of categories.

Popular Irish names foreigners can pronounce:

TARA: Meaning 'a hill in Meath'.

DARRAGH: Meaning 'fruitful'.

CLODAGH: Meaning 'a river in Tipp'.

FINN: Meaning 'fair or bright'.

CONOR: Meaning 'lover of hounds' (in a platonic way).

Popular Irish names foreigners can't pronounce:

TADHG: Meaning 'a poet'.

SAOIRSE: Meaning 'freedom'.

OISÍN: Meaning 'young deer'.

CAOIMHE: Meaning 'precious'.

SADHBH: Meaning 'sweet'.

Unpopular Irish names Irish people can't pronounce:

AOIDHGHEAN: Meaning 'born of fire'.

FLAITHBHEARTACH: Meaning 'lordly in action'.

MAOLANAITHE: Meaning 'devotee of the storm'.

TUATHFLAITH: Meaning 'princess of the people'.

ECHMHÍLIDH: Meaning 'horse-soldier'.

And then, finally, there are the unpopular names that everyone can pronounce but still no one wants to use.

GOBNAIT: May well mean 'piece of meat caught in the back of your throat'.

NiCKNAMES

Nicknames are a common feature of both rural and urban life, with many Irish men and women either blessed, born or cursed with nicknames growing up, some of which continue to be passed on from generation to generation. The following are a selection. To begin with, every town or village should have one of the following:

Spud: A name that is passed from eldest son to eldest son, of which no one knows the true origin. Generally, a daecent skin who does odd jobs around the town. More often than not, Spud's surname will be Murphy.

Dicey: Another name passed from father to son. Diceys are almost always very jolly individuals except on the football pitch when they play full-back and plough into any man giving their corner-backs a hard time.

Rasher: Surname does not have to be Bacon, but it helps. This character is usually a solid if not spectacular young man, who, alongside Dicey, is amongst the first to be pencilled into the starting fifteen. Interestingly, 58% of people called Rasher eventually become members of An Garda Síochána.

Next up, every town and village should have several animal related nicknames, which can include:

Spider: A friendly character who seems to have a hand in everyone's business yet no one says a bad word about him.

The Bull: While the Bull doesn't have to be the guy who owns a piece of land near the edge of a cliff, in all likelihood, he will be a thick-headed so-and-so who's particularly belligerent after a half-dozen pints of Guinness. Strangely enough, he will never fail to help old ladies across the road.

Froggy: A likeable sort who has forever got some deal or bit of business going on. As a result, he will succeed in the most unlikely of places. Made for *Dragon's Den*.

The Cat: The village goalkeeper, the son of the village goal-keeper, the grandson of the village goalkeeper. Or the French art thief who buys Hamlet cigars in the local shop.

Next up are the descriptive nicknames of which a village will have several.

Butsy: Tough, durable guy who you can count on during a war, but sometimes struggles during peacetime.

Hairy: A hard one to pinpoint, as there are bald men who have been called 'Hairy', but it seems to stem from the fact that at one stage in their ancestral past one of their forefathers had exceptionally long hair.

Horny: Pretty self-explanatory, really.

Red: This usually refers to someone with striking straw-berry-blonde (red) hair who is prone to bouts of fury, particularly on the football field.

And then finally there are the **-y, -een** and **-o** families of nicknames. Unbeknownst to most people, these final three groups have been locked into a bloody nickname turf war that has been going on for generations. As a result, it is likely that only one of these groups will be present in every town and townland.

The first two families in these groups are the **'-ys'** and the **'-eens'**. The **'-ys'** (or **'-ies'**) are led by one of Ireland's top dogs – Paddy – and also contain the likes of Robbie, Danny and Paulie. The **'-eens'** (or **'-íns'**) are led by Seanín, with henchman including Dansheen, Michilín and Podgeen. Both families have waged a long and protracted conflict as they seek to control whole counties, with particular attention turned to the profitable and ever-popular Munster nickname market.

An uneasy peace that developed between both parties was finally broken in the 1980s with the rise of the final family of nicknames, the **'-os'**, led by Dublin-based brothers Anto and Deco and including Briano, Steo and Neilo. Having gained control of the capital, over the last couple of decades their influence has begun to reach out past the suburbs into the commuter belt, setting off yet another chain of battles over what people should put at the end of their names.

FRiENDS

'There are no strangers, only friends you have not met yet.' – W.B. Yeats. While this old Irish adage is not one for an internet safety class for kids, it does point to that Irish characteristic of quickly making friends and inviting them to our wedding. There are many types of friends in Ireland.

- **Hun:** A favourite city term, particularly amongst women about their female friends. Huns share absolutely everything with each other except their fellas.

- **Skin:** While these might not be your closest friends, a 'decent ol' skin' will still be there for you if called on for a favour.

- **Scan:** Western term for a male friend in that 'we're just male friends' type of way, not that there is anything wrong with male friends.

- **Horse:** Regularly proceeded by 'howiya', 'horse' is a friendly description usually employed in the country for mates who are big enough to play full-back, centre-back or midfield.

🪝 **Buddy:** As in 'howiya buddy?' A good-humoured friend.

🪝 **Lad:** Though it might sound a little informal in some parts to be greeted by 'howiya lad', as you go further west this simply means, 'hey, friend'.

🪝 **Bro:** American import that became popular during the '90s when we all watched *Friends*.

🪝 **Cara:** Irish word meaning friend, which is a big favourite for when you are finishing an email to a mate who has recently emigrated, as in 'Anyway, I trust you won't get sunburnt and hope to see you again for a few pints at Christmas. Do chara, Ronan'. You can also use it as you sign off a final letter, as in '... and make sure someone looks after and walks Toby. I best be going now before the weather closes in entirely, please God I'll reach the South Pole by sunset. Do chara, Ronan.'

🪝 **Mate:** Just like overseas, this is one of the most common terms blokes use today about their male friends.

🪝 **Butty:** Not a sandwich involving sausages, chips or butter (though it can be), rather a friend you've had since you were small enough to have only one pair of pants that didn't have holes at the knees.

OTHER NAMES

Other names you might come across in Ireland are those that don't actually refer to a specific person.

TOM FOOLERY: Not the ol' man who lives down the lane with the dog with different-coloured eyes, but silly carry-on as identified by your history teacher who is threatening to ring your parents.

JO MAXI: This is not the name of the Yoruba taxi driver from southwest Nigeria whose given name is Stephen but whose Nigerian name you don't understand. Instead, Jo Maxi is the actual taxi. Get it?

DANIEL DAY: This refers to the Luas line and comes either from the fact that Daniel Day-Lewis is rumoured to have spent six months driving the Red Line from Tallaght to Connolly in preparation for a Hollywood blockbuster about a tram driver, or the fact that his surname bears a striking resonance to this particular form of public transport.

REILLY: While you might not know Reilly, you'll probably know of the 'life of Reilly', which reflects the easy-going life that many an Irish teenager enjoys and of which their father never fails to remind them of. The phrase is believed to have come from America, but if it's a Reilly you can be sure his father was from here.

HOLY JOE: Someone who is religious but not very Christian and is always giving out about the carry-on of young people today.

BOLLICKY BILL: The type of guy who is pure awkward and always wants to do the opposite of what everyone else wants to do. If you end up in a crap pub for your Christmas staff party and wonder why you're there, it's because 'Bollicky Bill' refused to go anywhere else.

NOT-NiCE PEOPLE

Once you get to know people's names it is then important to understand what sort of people they are. The first group to be understood in Ireland are those people in the community who are particularly unpleasant.

... Begrudgers: King of all the not-nice people in Ireland are the 'begrudgers'. 'Begrudgers' are those who practise 'begrudgery', an ancient Irish custom first invented to stop people feeling too smug about themselves, but which has changed to become something that allows people who feel they haven't achieved anything to complain about those who have. Begrudgers love giving out about someone who has done well and explaining why **a.** 'the person is really only a bollix', **b.** 'anyone could do that' or **c.** 'they're probably only doing it for a reason'. While in the past you would only meet begrudgers propping up the bar on a Friday, of late they have moved en masse onto social media.

... Old Biddies: Much like black holes whose gravitational pull is so strong it actually sucks in light, the gravitational pull of 'Old Biddies' is so powerful no rumour or scandal

can evade their nosiness. Unlike black holes, where light disappears never to return, once Old Biddies find a rumour about so-and-so carrying on with yer wan, they then project the news back out to the rest of the community to tut-tut over.

... Wagon: Though often mixed up with Old Biddies, 'wagons' are an entirely different species altogether. 'Wagons' do not spread or tolerate rumours but are simply just cranky, cantankerous old women who have the people skills of an influenza outbreak. The only creatures that get on with wagons are cats.

... Bollixes: Primarily used for the male of the species, 'bollixes' make up 64% of all the not-nice male people. These are the men who don't let you pull out during a traffic jam, answer their mobile phone in the cinema and expect to get served from the back of a queue.

... Weapon: Usually associated with an older woman, but someone who is a 'right weapon' is exceptionally dangerous and should not be crossed or cornered. Many a scurrilous rumour has been started by a weapon.

... Battle-axe: While a 'battle-axe' also refers to an older woman who should not be crossed, unlike wagons they are actually amenable to human contact and are very protective of people they love. Weapons would never dream of spreading a rumour about the loved one of a battle-axe because they know that it would end in tears during the middle of Sunday mass.

... Pox: Not the worst person in the world, but you wouldn't want to be hanging out with them for anything over a minute.

... Pox bottle: First cousin of a pox, 'pox bottles' often started out as schoolyard friends in primary school until they thought they were better than you.

RESPECTABLE TYPES

The following are the sorts of people you'd want with you in any mission behind enemy lines.

Head buck-cat: The leader of any group who can always be counted on to make all key decisions.

Hard-chaws: Every group needs at least one 'hard chaw' who never quits and who no one wants to mess with.

Hoors: Or, more specifically, a 'cute hoor'. These people are guaranteed to find all the shortcuts to get the job done quicker for more money and less work.

THOSE STUPID TYPES

While the Irish are a very intelligent group of people, as evidenced by some of the things its citizens have invented (the submarine, the hypodermic syringe, the Beaufort Scale, Sudocrem) we are not without our idiots, and boy do we have a lot of names for them!

Amadán: One of only two insults we learned in Irish growing up. This tends to refer to that particular type of idiot who parks in the disabled spot because he is only going into the shop for a minute.

Ludramán: The other Irish insult we learned growing up is employed for those young men in the village who were arrested by the Gardaí because they thought it would be a good idea to borrow the school bus.

Amlóg: The Irish insult that got away. This lesser-known slur refers to a silly woman usually identified by the fact that their car mirror is reflecting themselves rather than the road.

Eejit: The didn't-really-mean-anything-by-it lad who is suspended for the week because it was his idea to give birthday bumps to the incoming first years until one of them ended up in A&E.

Gobshite: Obnoxious individuals who really get on your nerves. They see the problems in everything but no solutions, and usually like the sound of their own voices. They think they are great and are never ever wrong, especially on Twitter.

Muppet: Those who hang off the gobshite's shoulder and laugh at all his jokes.

Daw: You know the person who is always standing in the way of everyone at football matches with his mouth wide open?

Gobdaw: You know the person who is always standing in the way of everyone at football matches and who can't keep his mouth shut?

Spanner: A guy who is always making stupid mistakes like leaving the cubicle door unlocked, dropping his phone into a pint or forgetting to bring his key out with him. Avoid taking his phone call any time after midnight.

Ginnit: In the southeast they use 'ginnit' as a polite way of saying 'asshole'. The rest of the country didn't know there was a polite way of calling anyone an asshole.

Lummox: A very strong but not very bright individual who's great for pulling a plough but not great at asking why the horse isn't doing it instead.

Dipstick: A quite well-liked individual who just happens to be known for his habit of filling his diesel car up with petrol.

Langer: While 'langers' can be found throughout the country, the greatest concentration of them can be found in Cork. Though langers are fine for playing five-a-side with, they are also the types who come up to you drunk on a night out and won't leave you alone. Unless you immediately tell them to 'Go away, ya langer', they will mess up what little chance you had of chatting up yer wan.

Thick: To give them their proper title, these are 'pure thicks' who are responsible for messing up 16% of nights out before they have even got going. Usually they achieve this by slagging off a mate of yours or by saying something pure thick about your new dress.

Bodhrán: Inoffensive individual who is always the last to be picked for a table quiz team.

Lula (Loolah): The type of person who does something stupid over and over and over again. All of us have lived with people like this who forget to lock the door on the way out, constantly go to bed with the fish fingers still cooking in the oven and are the reason the ESB bill is hitting a fifth consecutive high because they can't remember to turn off the electric shower in the morning.

Moron: Pretty much the same as above, except they tend to say something stupid over and over and over again. This something stupid will most likely be sexist, racist, ageist, dentist or some other word ending in -ist. Their saving grace, however, is that they don't realise that what they are saying is mildly offensive and are also the type of person who will always help someone whose car has broken down.

Gom: The type of person who is always saying the wrong thing at the wrong time.

Gombeen: The type of person who is always doing the wrong thing at the wrong time.

Gombeenman: The type of person who is always doing and saying the wrong things at the wrong time. An interesting fact in relation to the 'gom' family is that in every village you usually have to have at least three goms, two gombeens and one gombeenman.

Tulip: The type of person who always leaves the gate open and is responsible for half of the annual farm machinery breakdowns.

Tool: As well as being responsible for the other half of all annual farm machinery breakdowns, tools have the incredible skill of torpedoing a family reunion by accidentally saying something that starts an argument.

Gowl: While employed across Munster and in other pockets across the land, gowl, sometimes written 'gabhal', is often considered to Limerick what langer is to Cork. Quite simply, an idiot of the highest order.

Bungalow: Having nothing upstairs. This is used to describe the type of person who thinks it's great craic to hurl conkers at passing cars.

Full shilling: For some reason, no one is ever referred to as the full shilling. Instead, it is only brought up when someone is not the full shilling, in the same way they might be 'a few sangwiches short of a picnic' or 'a Mars Bar short of a selection box'.

THOSE YOU FEEL SORRY FOR TYPES

Those people you kind of feel a little bad for when you see them on the street.

- **Bleedin' tick:** Associated with though not exclusive to Dublin, 'bleedin' ticks' are those people who are adept at being totally inept, always putting the foot in the wrong place. A lot of people went out with a bleedin' tick when they were fifteen and have regretted it ever since.

- **Sap:** Someone who has little or no sense and doesn't realise what they are doing is usually inappropriate.

- **Innocent boy:** A sweet, quiet and entirely naïve boy. Brings his cousin to his debs because no one else would say yes. Last to be invited to a party and the person no one wants to sit beside in class. Will eventually put all this behind him to start up a tech company that is floated on the NASDAQ, making him wealthier than Longford.

- **Créatúr:** Or, as your mother always referred to him, the 'poor créatúr' that every village used to have. Growing up you never knew why he was a poor créatúr but guessed it might have had something to do with the gaunt, haunted expression he used to wear that made him look like a really sad marathon runner.

- **Scoby:** Originating from the acronym of a symbiotic culture of bacteria and yeast, this person used to skip health classes in school, which may explain why the last free seat on the bus was always beside them.

THOSE
iMMORAL TYPES

People who are associated (rightly or wrongly) with immoral behaviour, including those most likely to **do the dirt*** on you.

Wurrum: A boyfriend, soon to be ex, who cheats on you and then comes up with a ridiculous excuse like 'I was drunk', 'she kissed me' or 'I thought we were on a break'.

Dirt bird: This is the girl your boyfriend cheated with and she knowing you were going out together!

Toe-rag: Another man who can't be trusted, so don't be surprised when he admits to having an affair with the child-minder/babysitter/office temp/milkman.

Louser: He is the person who is cheating on your mate.

*Do the dirt: cheat.

Floozie: Yer wan who yer mate's boyfriend went off with. Would you believe that from the late '80s to the millennium there was a statue actually celebrating this type of behaviour on Dublin's main thoroughfare!

Trot filly, trot foal: Saying someone is their mother's daughter might in other circumstances be a compliment, but not in this case.

Strap: This is the term for a particularly impudent young woman. While a strap was something to be feared by those in authority, usually nuns, for many others they occupied a soft spot, more so when they were a character on the silver screen.

Hussy: Add a little immorality to the impudence of a strap and you get a hussy. Every town and village had one growing up. Also known as a 'brazen little hussy'. However, now that we have come out of 1950s Catholic Ireland, we realise these girls weren't hussies at all, but just confident young women who had chosen to reject the shackles of patriarchy.

THOSE FECK-ALL CRAIC TYPES

The type of people you wouldn't want to go for a pint with or spend a bus journey to Letterkenny with.

Dry shite: These people are absolutely zero craic. Dry shites could be childhood friends but that doesn't stop them from pouring cold water on your plan to gatecrash that house party or giving you half a dozen reasons why going on a spur-of-the-moment road trip will be a disaster.

Pain in the arse: These individuals are not mean-hearted, but just seem to find a way to say something that is uncalled for, unwarranted or uninteresting.

Creep: In fairness to the Irish creep, he doesn't really mean it and is never the quiet next-door type who buries people under his decking. Instead he just still lives at home with his mother and wears the same leather jacket he got for his confirmation.

Drip: You usually don't know these people until you end up in conversation with them. What is worse is that it is usually you who initiated the chat when you felt sorry for the member of your friend's stag or hen that no one was talking to. This is not too bad if you are in a pub and you can shuffle around, but a real killer if you get snookered between them come dinnertime.

Dreep: A cross between a drip and a creep.

Dose: This is someone who is often related to you so must therefore be endured even if they are sitting beside you at a wedding. Doses are those who can't help but tell you about their latest conquest, get-rich scheme, gripe with the government or work-related bonus. Finally there are two categories of doses: the dose and the awful dose.

THOSE YOU CROSS THE ROAD TO AVOID TYPES

When it comes to groups of young men you don't want to see sitting on your wall, there is a sliding scale of misbehaviour that you can use to judge whether you can go outside and tell them to skedaddle or whether you should just ring the guards.

Gets: Cheeky gits who are only giving smart remarks.

Bouchals: Don't get off the footpath when they meet older people or mothers with prams.

Tykes: Let the air out of half the car tyres on your street.

Pups: Knick-knock at people's doors and throw litter about.

Curs: Older than pups and why you should always lock up your bike.

Boyos: Responsible for over 90% of the graffiti in town.

Buckos: The ones who will sit on your car and then give you the finger when you tell them to get off.

Gougers: Give hoodies a bad name and have a tendency to shoplift.

Bowsies: Can be observed drinking a few cans, shouting abuse at each other and peeing in your begonias.

Gurriers: Can be observed drinking a good few cans, shouting abuse at passers-by and pulling up your begonias.

Hooligans: Wouldn't hurt you but might set fire to your wheelie bin.

Blackguards: Not nice at all. Blackguards would knock an old lady over and keep walking. People are always giving out about them on Joe Duffy.

Scumbags: Ring the guards, quick!

LOVE

——

Though the Irish might not be as associated with love as the French, a little-known fact is that St Valentine now lives in Ireland – or at least his remains do, located in the Carmelite Church on Whitefriar Street in Dublin. St Valentine is of course renowned the world over for being the patron saint of romantics and lovers. Less well known is that he is also the patron saint of beekeepers and epilepsy! Go figure!

In Ireland, we continue to honour St Valentine on his annual day on 14th February, when thousands of people exchange tat they don't really want with each other and hope that even though it's a Tuesday they might just get the ride. Of course, this is jumping the gun, and before you can swap ridiculously expensive Valentine cards with each other you must first meet the 'one'. The following gives an insight into the stages on the road to true love and the language we need along the way.

GENDER

In order to meet someone, it is not a bad idea to find some people of the requisite gender you are after. The names for these can vary dramatically from place to place.

- **Lads:** Traditionally this was a term used exclusively for men, especially in the eastern half of the country. However, this has slowly changed as the Atlantic coast definition of lads, meaning both male and female, has migrated eastwards. As a result, if you're single and male and someone texts back to your question 'Who are ya out with?' with the response 'The lads', it might be a good idea to throw on some deodorant and comb the hair just in case.

- **Young wans:** While it might sound a little derogatory to some, this is a traditional east-coast term for a woman.

- **Sham:** Though sham is sometimes used for a friend or someone who hails from a particular town in a particular county, it is also a common term for a man.

- **Fella:** A very common term for a guy, as in 'Who's that fella over there?'

Girdel: Sounds like the stage between a girl and a lady but is in fact just a strange way some people in Munster say girl.

Cub: Northern term for a young man which is neither negative nor positive – unless they want it to be.

Juck: North-western term for a boy.

FINDING SOMEONE OF INTEREST

Having arrived into a place with a large number of potential mates, the next step is finding someone who piques your interest. To this end, a number of approaches can be employed. What is interesting about all of these terms is how all of them sound like activities that a stalker might engage in.

ON THE LOOK-OUT: Sounds like you're either in danger or in search of your next victim. And you know what, maybe you are!

ON THE PROWL: Might make you feel like you're a leopard carefully negotiating the jungle, but in reality you're some randomer holding a half-bottle of Budweiser at the bar, homing in on a girl who has become separated from her friends.

ON THE HUNT: Once again that similarity between meeting the love of your life and tracking down prey!

ON THE LURK: Kind of like on the prowl, except yer man with the Budweiser is hiding behind a pillar just off the dance floor.

ON THE PULL: Perhaps the least sociopathic sounding of these terms, 'on the pull' simply explains the exercise of meeting someone in a way that sounds exceptionally labour-intensive.

TERMS OF ATTRACTiON

Once the prospective man or woman has been identified and not scared off, it is no harm to understand what they look like. While this generally has absolutely no influence on how you approach them, it can help you when you are describing them to a friend.

Ride: Multi-gender, this word refers to a man or woman of immeasurable good looks. While it does not take a long stretch of the imagination to understand what it refers to, the word itself is strangely inoffensive.

Stunner: Referring almost solely to the female sex, a woman who is described as a stunner is generally considered to be out of the league of 98% of the men who use the term, which is a pity, because if you just went over and talked to her …

A bit of all right: Meaning drop-dead gorgeous for either sex.

Beour: While it might sound like something that you'd find exhibited at an agricultural show, a 'beour' is actually a beautiful woman. It is most common in the southern parts of the country.

Fine thing: Meaning beautiful, this can refer to both a man or a woman, or for that matter a car, a bullock or a ride-on lawnmower.

Bure: Again, we are not at an agricultural show, but still in Munster, with a 'bure' being the male equivalent of a 'beour'.

Feen: Feens are like bures, but are found mostly in Connacht. There are reports that in certain parishes of the west a 'feen' is used to describe an undesirable young man, but sure aren't the bad ones always undesirable!

Buck: The same as feens, used also in Connacht and Donegal. What sets 'bucks' apart from feens is that a feen usually leans back on the bar expecting an approach, while a buck tends to lean forward.

Feek: One of those multi-meaning words that refer to a lovely lady.

CHAT-UP LINES

Once the object of your affection has been identified, the next stage is getting to know them, something that can only be done properly by what older people used to refer to as 'talking'. One equally old way this can be initiated is through a chat-up line, a verbal proposal that the person being spoken to can swipe either left or right. While many of these lines have been employed the world over, in Ireland we do have a few of our own.

I HAVE ROAD FRONTAGE: While declaring that you own land (or more specifically your Dad does) that borders a road is pretty much as close to Gordon Gecko you can get in Connacht, or Munster for that matter, this chat-up line was surprisingly successful during the Celtic Tiger years. It showed balls. It showed confidence. And, if you were honest, and not the second-eldest son, then it also showed you had a good chance of getting planning permission.

WOULD YOU LIKE TO BE BURIED WITH MY PEOPLE?: Sometimes viewed as the poor man's 'road frontage', this chat-up line is both humble and mildly disturbing. At the very least it is important if you are ever asked this question to first find out whether he is talking literally or metaphorically.

CAN I SEE YOU HOME?: Part polite, part forward, 'Can I see you home' is at its most romantic when he knows that your parents will both be still up watching the end of *The Late Late Show*. If he knows you live alone in a bedsit then I'd suggest just allowing him to see you to the cloakroom, and saving the walk home until the second date.

HAVE YOU GOT A LIGHT?: While there is hardly a more universal chat-up line than 'have you got a light?', it enjoys a special place in Irish hearts. This is due to the fact that Ireland was the first country in the world to ban smoking in pubs, which forced a swathe of people away from loud music and their friends, who never liked them anyway. This allowed a whole cohort of young men and women the opportunity to race outside and use this question as the perfect conversation starter. That half of these people didn't actually smoke or have a cigarette with them was immaterial.

WOULD YOU DANCE WITH MY FRIEND?: A favourite in the era of slow sets and juvenile discos, this brought a whole generation together until they broke up two weeks later at the next disco.

WOULD YOU LIKE A MINERAL?: If you don't know what a mineral is, don't worry, this line hasn't been used since the moon landings – but it sure sounds cute.

I PLAY GAA: This chat-up line is quite site-specific, increasing in popularity in heavily urbanised areas, particularly those close to Coppers.

DO YOU LIKE CHEESE? BECAUSE I'M AN EASI SINGLE: One of the only proper chat-up lines that has a rate of return that was marginally better than those charity lottery cards they sell outside supermarkets.

KiSSiNG

If your opening line does not crash and burn, then your chances of romance have jumped dramatically. You now need to capitalise on this early spadework and endear yourself enough to them that either by the next slow song or the following date you might be able to move in for a kiss. While they say the French have a multitude of words for kissing, in fairness to Ireland we are not found lacking in that department either. It's just that most of our words do not sound as romantic.

♥ **Shifting:** What most Irish people's first kiss turned out to be. If 'shifting' sounds as tender as a garage clear-out, it is probably because that's about how tender it actually was. With teeth gnashing and enough saliva swapped to shock an epidemiologist, reversing fork-lifts have looked more romantic than two young teenagers kissing. Thankfully, the art of kissing improves as people get older, even if the word we use for it remains the same.

♥ **Scoring:** At one stage this word was the source of much controversy in certain parts of Ireland due to the fact that about half the country took scoring to mean kissing, while the other half presumed it meant getting all the way to home base, which was all the more surprising considering most young men didn't even know what or where second or third base were!

♥ **Meet:** An old way you got your friend to ask a girl to kiss you. 'Would you meet my friend?', they'd say as you leant against the wall, nonchalantly holding your Club Orange.

♥ **Feek:** Just like score, 'feek' could mean different things to different people in different places. However, for the most part it meant a good old snog.

♥ **Get off with:** Sounds as amorous as someone disembarking a bus, but what many a young lad or lassie were asked on a Monday morning: 'So did you get off with them?'

♥ **Click:** To hear that two people 'clicked' today suggests that they have found something in common like Chilean wine, indie movies or an interest in dry-stock farming. A generation ago 'to click' was to hook up with someone, with kissing being the least of it.

♥ **Lob the gob:** Without a doubt this must be the most unromantic way to kiss anyone, anywhere in the world. Not even farm animals kiss like this, but it doesn't stop colleagues and classmates asking each other if they 'lobbed the gob' over the weekend.

DATING

Once the awkward first lines are over, and presuming the kissing was a success (and you've passed muster with their friends), the next part of love is dating, for which there are several terms you can employ.

- **Going out with:** By far the most common term we use in Ireland, even if 73% of Irish couples don't know where they want to go out to.

- **Seeing someone:** While it might sound like someone regaining consciousness, 'I'm seeing someone' was how most relationships started out before parents were ever told who that person was.

- **Doing a line:** A nice quaint term mostly used a generation ago. It often meant that you were dating someone but it wasn't that serious because you were due to get the boat to England next week to look for work.

- **Stepping out:** Another old favourite in the days of dance halls, showbands and Catholic Church surveillance.

TERMS OF ENDEARMENT

If the dating proves consistent, then we call that a relationship. Well done. At this stage, you will need some terms of endearment for each other. Here are a few Irish suggestions, beginning with the old ways, from the days when love was expressed in ballads.

Agraw machree (a grá mo chroí): Anyone who calls their loved one this probably smokes a pipe, has a lifetime subscription to *Ireland's Own* or died in the 1960s.

Acushla: There is a chance you are also already dead, but take some heart in knowing that your love for your dear was so strong it has been committed to verse.

Ahaskey: This has dipped in popularity since its heyday when it was widely employed in the letters home from Irish potato-thieving convicts in Van Diemen's land.

Me darling: The couple have already celebrated their silver anniversary and are not only still in love with each other but are still talking and sleeping in the same room!

Me love: An example to us all, you've been with each other through thick and thin, from Irish World Cup trips to rain-soaked summer holidays in Tramore. Fair play.

Me auld flower: Despite comparing your love to a decaying plant, this is a surprisingly sentimental way of referring to your one and only.

Musha: Your dear loved one who, even at 75, has your back.

The quare one: And they said Romantic Ireland was dead and gone!

Himself or herself: How you or others might describe your loved one. 'How's himself?' to which you might answer, 'Ah sure, he is himself'.

While we Irish make use of the modern ways people refer affectionately to their significant other – my love, babe, honey – we do have a few more indigenous ones.

Hun: While your husband or wife might also be a member of a group of Central Asian nomadic people that invaded

Europe in the 4th and 5th centuries, in all likelihood they aren't and you are just shortening the lesser-used 'honey' to 'hun'.

Darl: Another shortened version, this time of 'me darling'.

Luv: Multi-gender for your dearest, but then you guessed that, didn't you?

My better half: In fairness, if someone says this, they are usually right.

The other half: About as romantic as it sounds.

Squeeze: This relates to your love, although referring to them as your 'latest squeeze' might suggest that you are going to suffocate the life out of them (and the relationship) within the fortnight.

Me fella: If referring to your fella at home this is fine and simply refers to your long-term boyfriend. However, if you are introducing your boyfriend to others as 'me fella', you have most likely only recently begun going out and therefore are marking your territory by telling everyone to keep their hands and eyes off him.

My man: Very warm description of your love, which also indicates he can probably put up a shelf and knows when to put out the bins.

Me mot: Refers to your girlfriend and is a term that you should stop using once you get married, have children or cease being a teenager.

NiGHTS OUT

—

The weekend is a big part of Irish life and at its heart is often the local pub. Of course, there are other things to do at the weekend like ... er ... other stuff not involving the pub. Thankfully, though, if you do happen to get caught up doing this other stuff, you can still go to the local during the week. That works too. Whenever you do get caught in the gravitational pull of the local it can be handy to have the lingo to go with it.

GOING OUT-OUT

The first thing you need to decide when heading to the pub is what sort of night you are planning on. Knowing this will help you decide whether you need five minutes and a blast of deodorant to get ready or three hours, two bottles of wine and your best friends in tow to gossip about the week. There is a whole spectrum of possibilities.

JUST THE ONE (JUST THE WAN): Going for 'just the one' might be as difficult as herding cats, but this is perhaps the most popular type of pub visit. More on this later.

AWAY OUT: Probably just a couple of pints because you've got work in the morning.

GOING OUT-OUT: The Big Daddy of Irish nights out. Get the make-up on, use your brother's expensive eau du toilette, make sure your briefs are clean and your socks are matching as all systems are go and you won't be home until the wee hours.

HEADING OUT: If someone asks you if 'you're interested in heading out', while they might not say where they are intending on 'heading out to' – the zoo, the art museum, the garden centre – it can be safe to assume that they mean to the pub. Yes is always a good answer.

FLOATING OR BUZZIN': 'Let's float out' or 'are you buzzin?' are just two new examples of 'heading out' for the new millennials.

HITTING THE TILES: Naggin in the handbag, new dress on, old boyfriend forgotten about, taxi booked and you'll be walking home holding those heels in no time.

INTO TOWN: Hard to tell with this one. While it usually means something like a movie with a quick pint afterwards, don't be surprised if you end up staying out all night and thinking it's a good idea to catch an early morning ferry to France.

OUT ON THE LASH: You'll find me in a ditch tomorrow morning.

OFF ON THE BEER: A stag weekend where it's likely that at least one member of the party will need to be bailed out.

TO BE ON THE RIP OR THE TEAR: Like rolling a hand grenade into the weekend, this is a recipe for a crazy one. Wouldn't be a bad idea to ring ahead and make a reservation in A&E.

TO BE ON THE SAUCE: Very like 'to be on the rip' except a little less chaotic and a little more prolonged.

OFF THE WAGON: Not good at all. Lock up the brake fluid and organise a search party if you aren't back by Wednesday.

DESCRIBING THE VENUE

Another deciding factor as to whether you should go out or into a particular pub is the size of the crowd already there. When describing how busy a particular pub, club or indeed any other place is, Irish people prefer to substitute people per square metres with more colourful accounts.

— **Dead:** One man and his dog. And they could be the ones working behind the bar.

— **Half-empty:** Between two and six people. They are probably watching darts on the TV and will turn to look at you when you come in. Reverse, reverse, reverse!

— **Daecent:** Reasonable crowd. A decent amount of people. Enough to keep the bar in business but don't think you will be able to have a discreet conversation without everyone noticing.

— **Buzzin':** An ideal crowd. Plenty of familiar faces, great energy in the room, space at the bar and there's always a urinal/cubicle free. Happy days.

— **Busy:** A large crowd. Not much chance that you'll find seats but you'd still expect to get served in a reasonable time.

— **Jammers (or jam-packed):** Very big crowd. What pubs were like on Dawson Street on a Tuesday night during the boom. Jammers means that while you might get to the bar okay you can be sure the queue for the toilet is in the double digits.

— **Heaving:** A large crowd. It'll probably take you 15 minutes to walk to and from the smoking area and good luck trying to carry those three pints back from the bar. Great atmosphere though!

— **Black:** Serious crowd. You'll find it impossible to walk but are instead lifted along with the crowd. Impossible to find anyone you know but that's fine because you'll end up finding people you don't know. Anyone who has seats came in more than four hours ago, if not the day before, and are despised by everyone else. Comes from the Irish 'dubh le daoine' – literally, black with people.

— **Hangin' from the rafters:** Huge crowd. Enough money is made from the cloakroom on nights like this to put a child through college.

— **Sweat box:** Ridiculous crowd. Can't get your hands out of your pockets. The only person you have a hope of chatting up is the person who's stuck next to you.

— **Mental:** massive crowd. Breaking all health and safety guidelines, the temperature generated in the centre of this mass of people is roughly similar to the Earth's core.

JUST THE ONE

'Just the one' is rarely 'just the one', but it doesn't mean we don't persist in using it. In fact, so determined we are to go out and only have one drink we have a selection of phrases to describe it.

Just the one: The most popular recognition of our desire to have only one drink. Unfortunately, 76% of people who say this as they head out the door will inevitably find themselves still at the bar at a quarter to one, with a shot in one hand and a concession for the local nightclub in their other. 'Just the one, me hole' they'll be told the next morning!

A pint: As well as people saying they are 'going for a pint' you will also have those who will say they are 'going for a **quick pint**' and those who say they are 'going for **A** pint', with the latter signifying they understand the risk that one pint will become three, which will become five, which will become a phone call to the office in the morning to say they've a dose and won't be able to make it in.

A quick one: This is the post-work/swift catch-up with an old friend/waiting for the bus home/before the curtains go up/shortly before kick-off/just to be social pint.

Head in for a jorum: Old-time phrase for the one pint.

A jar: Particularly popular drink between two old buddies on a Thursday night.

A gargle: Not to be mixed up with that pink liquid your dentist offers you after a cleaning, 'a gargle' is what you and your colleagues have immediately after work on a Friday.

A couple of scoops: Fine, it's more than one, but when the scoop is usually a Guinness then you can have two and still call it one (except in court).

PARTiES

What often makes a good night out into a great night out is the resulting party that can emerge from it, either at home, in the pub or in the GAA function room, which can feel like both. While not all of these parties are planned, some of them are, and knowing what distinguishes one from the other can be useful if you ever get more than one invite.

★ **Prinks:** Strictly speaking, this is the pre-night out party that takes place in preparation. Prinks, meaning 'pre-drinks' has increased in popularity, partly due to the increased cost of drinks on a night out and partly due to the growing amount of time it actually takes some to get ready for a night out.

★ **Session:** 'A session' or 'a sesh' is perhaps the best type of party. However it is impossible to be invited to one as they never start out as sessions. Instead they start out as a couple of drinks as you watch the football. It is only by a strange quirk of fate (the unexpected arrival of an old friend, a surprise invite to a house party or it being Friday) that it turns into a session and you finish the night or early morning hugging your best friend and telling him 'I love you, man'.

★ **Hooleys:** Usually a pre-planned party that involves Irish song, dance, music and lots of men shouting 'hup ya boyo!' Hooleys seem to operate under a law of their own and can last for several hours (even days) after other pubs and clubs are forced to shut.

★ **Céilidh:** A céilidh is similar to a hooley in that it is a coming together for a night of singing, drinking and dancing. Someone always traipses the floor finding partners for everyone, so a large, rarely choreographed jig can be carried out. In certain parts of the country, particularly up north, a céilidh often refers to a night of chat, craic and laughter in someone's house, so best to check which one before you don that Hawaiian shirt.

★ **Hop:** If you're off to a 'hop', then it is 1955 and you and Marty McFly are starring in *Back to the Future*, the Irish version. More commonly known as a 'dance', the 'hop' used to be the place to have two bottles of stout before you got up and met the woman of your dreams who would share your life, farm and eventually produce half a dozen Irish Catholic children.

★ **Shindig:** When extended family members come home from Australia, America and prison to re-unite, share stories, sing semi-autobiographical ballads and then argue about who was really responsible for breaking the telly all those years ago.

★ **Do:** Any one of a number of events that are attended by your family, your neighbours and anyone else your mother asked in the village. Nearly always takes place in the function room of the local pub/hotel/GAA club with vegetable soup mandatory.

★ **Piss-up:** This often involves little people (these are not the ones drinking!) in white dresses or little leather jackets with crucifixes pinned onto them, otherwise known as Communion parties.

★ **Lock-in:** Even more elusive than a session, the lock-in is something you don't go to but get trapped in. Of course, feeling that you're 'trapped' is only based on whether you think staying in a bar after hours with half a dozen other regulars to drink pints with until dawn is a bad thing or not.

★ **Bender:** If someone invites you out on a bender, for the love of God, say no! This is the type of session that ends political careers, destroys marriages and results in you standing in court trying to explain why you were found asleep naked in the penguin enclosure of Dublin Zoo.

CALLING iT A NiGHT

If you find yourself on any of these nights out and need to leave, there is a variety of phrases you might use.

I'm going to head off: You've had the exact number of pints you promised yourself, no more, no less, so it's time to leave. Not to be mixed up with 'I'm going to head on' where the person is heading to the next pub which he or she feels will be more craic.

I'm calling it a night: Very strong-willed of you as you head out the door five minutes after the match you were watching with friends has finished. Your friends will probably call you a dry shite and blame your new girlfriend for this.

I better hit the road: Usually the person saying this has a bit of a distance to walk/amble/stumble before they arrive home.

I'm away off: A bit more common in the country where there is a good chance that the person leaving is a farmer who needs to check the cattle when he gets home.

I'll be back in a minute: ... and then don't come back. This works perfectly for stag nights, when no one will notice. This statement will often generate a knowing smile from another new Dad who also just wants to go back to the hotel and enjoy a good night's sleep. Doesn't work if there are just two of ye.

DRINK QUANTITIES

When ordering drinks in Ireland, understanding quantities of drink can be helpful, if only to understand why it is you have such a hangover the next morning.

A PINT: The standard measurement of choice. For our American friends, it is important to note that an Irish pint is similar to that of an imperial pint, and at 568ml it's 100ml more than what you might order in up-state Oregon, so watch out for that.

A SHOT: On the other hand, our measure of spirits is nearly 9ml smaller than that of our American friends, so if you have as many pints as you have shots then it'll balance itself out by the end of the night, promise!

A NAGGIN: This is a 200ml bottle of spirits that has become the modern accoutrement for a cheap night out, particularly for younger and less selective drinkers. One interesting feature of the naggin is the sheer number and variety of ways it can be hidden when trying to gain entry into a nightclub. From the down the sock, in the jock or strapped tight across the belly, to hidden in the handbag, popped in the hair bun or employed in the bra, the naggin truly is the 'East-Berliner looking to escape' of Irish measures.

A FLAGON: There is really only one correct way to buy this two-litre bottle of cider and that is from the back of a van outside a music festival. As for a serving suggestion, we'd say warm. Not suggested for a night out.

DRUNK

Unfortunately, not all nights end after two pints and a bag of chips, with the Irish occasionally (just occasionally!) being known to drink to excess. While in truth the Irish probably drink as much or as little as most other nations, we do seem to have a shocking amount of words for when we have one too many.

- ◆ **Half cut:** The stage where chat-up lines no longer work because you keep messing up the punchline.

- ◆ **Langered:** Common after Irish sporting events overseas. Not sober enough to chat someone up but mildly amusing to foreigners.

- ◆ **Pissed:** The good-natured, lovable type of drunkenness often found around Christmas when you meet up with all your friends home from London.

- ◆ **Fluthered:** Drunk uncle at a wedding.

- ◆ **Bananas:** Easily identified by the fact that the person in question is now wearing a tie around his head and is urging others to join him on the table to dance.

- ◆ **Bollixed:** Serious hangover territory is being entered here.

- **Three sheets to the wind:** Walking home from the pub in the company of a traffic cone while singing 'On Raglan Road'.

- **Plastered:** Commonly witnessed amongst winners of the local junior hurling competition as they arrive with the cup (now missing a handle after being chucked across the road) into their eighth pub.

- **Stocious:** Found outside the nightclub chatting up a wheelie bin.

- **Jarred:** Only fit to be put in a taxi and sent home because they're being a complete eejit.

- **Scuttered:** The stage where any decent friend will take you home.

- **Shit-faced:** The stage where you are not allowed into a taxi and the same decent friend has to help you walk home instead.

- **In a hoop:** That's yer wan who was mad dancing earlier and shouting 'you're hot' at the band, and who is now asleep on the coats in the corner.

- **Fecked:** This is the person you had hoped would help you out later but who has had too much and is now of absolutely no use.

◆ **Rubbered:** When the person has lost all traces of personal space and is now chewing your ear as he talks to you.

◆ **Twisted:** Dangerous territory where you may drink-dial an ex or a person who will soon become your ex.

◆ **Wasted:** The reason you left your boyfriend sleeping on the couch at your friend's housewarming.

◆ **Locked:** The level of inebriation observed with younger drinkers.

◆ **Rat-arsed:** Nobody likes hanging out with you at this stage.

◆ **Paralytic:** What the HSE deals with on Fridays, Saturdays and Sundays.

◆ **Ossified:** What the HSE has to deal with after it deals with all those who were paralytic. Sigh.

HUNGOVER

Finally, it shouldn't come as a shock that for a country that has many an Irishism for the level of insobriety we also have several more for the level of suffering we endure the morning after.

THE FEAR: This is without doubt the most dreaded type of hangover going. 'The Fear' combines all the physical symptoms that indicate you were utterly twisted the night before – nausea, headache, fatigue and a little bit more nausea – with the growing realisation of just how much of a fool you actually were the night before. The very worst form of the Fear involves a partial blackout, where the survivors can't remember how much of a fool they actually were the night before. The Fear strikes worst after office Christmas parties, weddings and New Year's Eve parties.

I'M DYING: What you will hear from someone who is either about to throw up, go back to bed or both.

BANJOED: Not fit for anything at least until tomorrow.

I'M HANGING: This is where you are surviving, barely, and are just about capable of short conversations and being in company – but that's pretty much the height of it.

MY HEAD'S BANGIN': This one is focused purely on the headache, which is why they will be cradling their noggin like it's a Fabergé egg.

IN THE HORRORS: The type of hangover involving spirits and the fact that you had to come in to work or attend your niece's first birthday party the next day.

Two final hangover terms you might come across are 'the cure' and 'the hair of the dog'.

THE CURE: This is what some people occasionally go looking for the morning after the night before in order to fix their suffering. While the cure means certain things to certain people, by and large it is a drink that will bring an end to the hangover currently being endured. Widely regarded as the best cure is the hair of the dog.

THE HAIR OF THE DOG: This is also used across the water, is one of the earliest known remedies whereby the person suffering the hangover drinks a glass of whatever they were drinking the night before. This can occasionally prove problematic for those sessions where much uncertainty surrounds what exactly your best friend was buying you at the end of the night. While the hair of the dog is yet to undergo any proper scientific scrutiny despite many willing college-age volunteers, it doesn't stop people trying it at stag and hen weekends across the country.

TROUBLE
AND
DiSORDER

—

While Ireland is by and large a very friendly place to go out and about, it is not without its occasional spots of trouble and disorder. Of these there are several types.

TROUBLE

Hassle: While hassle can sometimes lead you to get anything from a scalp to a belt, by and large it simply causes annoyance and messes up your day/evening/night. Heavy rain, needing a lift to get home, your ex being in the same pub or forgetting your bank card at the check-out counter are all forms of hassle that you can do without.

Ruckus: In Ireland ruckus is what happens upstairs between siblings. If it gets out of control and parents have to shout 'where's all that ruckus coming from?' you might be in trouble.

Agro: Almost exclusive to towns and cities, 'agro' is short for aggression and the type of situation that, if not handled delicately, will result in a row. Agro can always be found outside chippers on Saturday nights.

Míle murder: This term means a big old fuss that doesn't have to result in a thousand murders. This type of furore was more common in the era of dance halls and drive-in movies (not that we really ever had drive-in movies).

Rí rá agus ruaille buaille: This all-Irish term is still employed for similar events as above though there is a hint of enjoyment to the phrase that means chaos and commotion. If you can avoid a black eye, these nights can be great fun.

Pure bedlam: Bedlam originally comes from the mental institution of St Mary of Bethleham in London which became known as Bedlam. In Ireland, however, we have our own special form of bedlam, which we call 'pure bedlam'. This can sometimes be observed in unsupervised secondary school classrooms, shopping centres on Christmas Eve and in regional A&E wards over the long weekend.

THREATS

Even before any trouble breaks out, quite often the threat of trouble and violence will occur. If you want to avoid such problems it is handy to understand the following terms.

- **I'll bate the head off ya!:** Very common threat during U-14 matches between opposite numbers. Thankfully, no one ever 'bates the head off' anyone, but that doesn't mean the phrase has failed to put many a corner-forward off their game.

- **I'll burst ye!:** And you know if he could only manage to catch ya he would!

- **After school!:** Said by a teacher it usually means evening study; said by that slightly disturbed looking lad who sits down the back of your art class it means something else entirely. Make sure you get to the lockers first or take the long way home.

- **What are you looking at?:** Sounds like a question, is actually a threat. Common in Dublin's Fair City, on hearing this you should turn 180 degrees and walk away.

- **Are you calling me a liar?:** What part of turning 180 degrees and walking away did you not understand? Considering you decided to engage in conversation by saying 'nothing' or, better yet, 'I wasn't looking at anything', you're on your own. If it were me I'd still contemplate that 180-degree turn but choose to run rather than walk.

- **I'll stop the car:** There was no greater threat to children messing in the backseat in the '80s than your mother telling you she'd 'stop the car' or, worse again, telling your Dad 'to stop the car'. This was in a time when you could stop a car anywhere at any time and know there were always little branches nearby you could break off and bring back to the car. Silence would always ensue.

FiGHTiNG

Though it doesn't happen as often as Kent Brockman and *The Simpsons* might have us believe, there are occasional brawls that take place in the country, which can be roughly categorised as follows.

Throwing shapes: This is where not one punch, dig or skite is thrown in anger but those involved dance around each other pretending they are going to start fighting.

Pushing and shoving: A little bit more aggressive than throwing shapes, but harmless all the same. Some people might lose a few buttons.

Handbags: Looks like a fight. Sounds like a fight. Hurts like a fight. But is in fact only 'handbags' which means that no one gets into trouble even if those involved finish with a black eye, bloodied nose and a trip to the dentist.

Mill-up: A great big scuffle where everyone is on top of each other, meaning not one clean punch is thrown.

Melee: Type of row that starts at the bar and spills out onto the road. You'll end up reading about this in the local paper the following week.

Free-for-all: Sounds like the best car-boot sale ever but is in fact one of those affairs where there is no real rhyme or reason to who is or isn't getting thumped.

Schmozzle: Drawing on characteristics of all of the above and then transferred onto the GAA pitch, this is what a fight on a football field is called. That one person was hospitalised for concussion and another needed stitches doesn't take away from the fact that because it was a 'schmozzle' and not a punch-up it was actually a bit of fun to watch, even if the commentators won't admit to it.

KNOCKS

Unfortunately, if you do get caught up in any of the previous types of trouble, disorder or fighting it might result in one of the following knocks.

TIP: What your big brother says when your mother comes home and you're crying: 'I only tipped him!' Equivalent to a 'thump' (see below).

THUMP: What your older brother really did to you (see 'tip' above) while your mother was at the shops. Level of impact reflects the sound of the word, 'THUMP!'

DIG: A 'dig' is a low-down punch in the stomach when they weren't expecting it. You might see this at football matches when the corner-forward gives the big midfield a 'dig' during a melee before disappearing away.

BELT: Usually employed when you get hit by something accidentally. This could be 'the belt' of a ball, sliothar or windy gate.

LAMP: This occurs when you experience a knock from something that is attached to the hand of someone swinging for you. For instance, you could get 'a terrible lamp' off a stick or a bar or indeed a lamp. Occasionally, if the person swinging for you has really long arms then they don't need to be holding anything and they can just lamp you unaided.

STEEVER: Usually refers to a kick up North, which thankfully refers to Ulster and not up the neither regions.

CLATTER: This is when you get a right knock, which is entirely accidental. Getting a 'clatter' can leave you very much the worse for wear and you will often need a decent amount of time to recover. Examples of it are often seen on the training field. For instance, if two lads 'clattered into each other' at least one will be concussed, or if you 'got a right clatter across the hand' at camogie there's a good chance you'll have some sort of fracture.

SKELP: What you get if you are caught raiding the slightly crazy old man's apple orchard down the lane from you.

SKITE: Kind of the same as above except the orchards you are raiding are up North.

PUCK: A blow usually presented with a closed fist as a once-off by some coward who then runs away. Also the type of punch the small corner-forward throws during a melee when the person receiving it isn't looking.

LAND: There are two types of 'lands' that you can get, 'the awful lands' and 'the right lands'. An 'awful land' is a non-physical land you get when you hear a terrible bit of news you hadn't expected, which can range from a death in the family to finding out someone left the handbrake off the family Corolla and it ended up rolling into the lake. 'A right land', on the other hand, is a knock that lies somewhere between a clatter and a belt in terms of intensity. Generally speaking, it usually involves something quite large like a bull or a garage door, but for some fortuitous reason you didn't receive the full force of it. As a result, you'll be back at work the following day.

LEATHER: Ask pre-1980s parents and Christian Brothers about this. Children back then were as much in fear of a 'leathering' as they were in fear of *Jaws*, the Boogieman and *Glenroe*.

SEAMUS: This was quite specific and referred to a dead leg that was usually imposed on you by someone two years ahead of you.

KICK THE SHITE OUT OF: Thankfully this expression is rarely followed through on but merely mentioned as what your uncle would do if he ever found out who was responsible for egging his door. If it was the egging of him then he might threaten to 'kick the living shite out of' you.

For many of these expressions you can add to the intensity of the blow by adding the following adjectives beforehand to create a sliding scale of upwards intensity.

A **SOLID** thump.

A **SERIOUS** thump.

An **ALMIGHTY** thump.

An **UNMERCIFUL** thump.

BEING ANNOYING

In understanding what can cause any one of these problems it can be important to look at some of the ways trouble can come about. One of these is by being annoying. To help you identify when you are in danger of doing this, the following phrases and what they mean might help.

- **Stoppit, will ya?:** You might like to have your girlfriend stroke your hair, but how many times does she have to tell you she doesn't like it!

- **Quit it!:** You are probably only six years old and your mother who has just got in from work is enjoying a nice cup of tea over an episode of *Countdown*. Just stop running across the couch for half an hour and go outside and play with a stick.

- **You're just being annoying now:** It was your fault we're late for dinner, stop trying to make up for it with a string of mediocre jokes.

- **You're doing my head in:** It's three hours to Cork and you are already beginning to whistle badly along with the radio? I mean seriously?!

- **You're really starting to get on my wick:** You're out for a pint with your friend who began the conversation by slagging off your football team for losing last weekend. It's now 20 minutes on and he is still going.

- **You're being pure scaldy:** When the person just can't drop a subject or keeps pestering you for information you don't want to share they are being 'pure scaldy' and are at risk of being told where to go.

- **You've my head wrecked:** What someone might say when they've been asked a 15th consecutive question which is as silly as the previous 14. This is used not for children under 10 but for loved ones who are giving you the second degree because you were late home yesterday evening.

- **You're starting to piss me off:** Don't immediately worry if a loved one says this to you, especially if you are only breathing. It might be that they are in the first trimester of pregnancy or their blood sugar level is really low and they just really need food.

- **You're annoying the f … out of me:** Also used about a significant other. However, because this is such a harsh thing to say to someone's face I would strongly suggest you just tell your best friend how your husband's constant desire to hang shelves and use power tools early on a Sunday morning is making you feel.

- **You're just plain annoying:** Though this might appear polite and restrained, if your girlfriend says this to you then you might want to start trying to remember your old password for Tinder. The reason for this is because 'you're just plain annoying' is code for 'I am disgusted by your presence and at a loss as to why I thought I wanted to go out with you in the first place.' Your relationship will be brown bread by the weekend.

GETTING ANGRY

While we Irish might like to think of ourselves as being a laid-back bunch of people (at least that's how we describe ourselves when dating online), there are occasions when we just get angry. Here are a number of ways this can happen, in ascending order of angriness.

Raging: Not as angry as you might think. How someone feels if they come back from the jacks and realise that Ryan Gosling had stopped by while they were in the queue. 'They're raging they missed it.'

Bulling: When something has unfairly gone against someone, like a free kick, a job interview or a court case. In such situations, little sense can be talked into them until they've calmed down.

Pure thick: Kind of the same as 'bulling' but generally what has gone against them was the correct decision. But Jaysus don't tell them that!

Effin' and blindin': The upset is still raw and the person is in the midst of processing the pain and anger by articulating it through the use of some awful profanities. Give them another couple of minutes.

Shouting and roaring: Sometimes called 'still shouting and roaring', this is the second stage of anger following 'effin' and blindin', where they have moved on from cursing to just yelling at the top of their voices.

Go bananas: This one is similar to going ballistic except you don't know what it is that set the person off and caused them to start trashing the place.

Lose the rag: What you might observe with those teachers who tend to be quite mild-mannered until a student doesn't have their homework done for the fifth consecutive day.

Fit to be tied: When a person discovers that someone, like a work colleague, has been getting an advantage over them such as bonuses, shorter shifts or their own parking space. And what is more, they've been getting this perk for nearly a year now!

Lose the head: No point even entertaining the idea of talking to this person. Remember how your junior manager reacted in last year's county final when five minutes from time, four points down, he saw his full-forward being sent off for retaliation? That's how someone loses the head.

Go ballistic: The reaction of someone when you accidentally let slip that you saw their boyfriend talking to yer wan late last night.

Lose the plot: This is dangerous territory wherein the person is not only very emotional, out of control and screaming, they also have one of the legs of the kitchen table in their hand and are using it to smash up the condiments!

GETTING INTO TROUBLE

If it is you who is responsible for causing all the ruckus, who was caught giving the dig or who let their anger get the better of them, then there is a fair to middling chance you'll get into trouble. Here are some types of Irish trouble.

~ **Caught rapid:** Though this is often associated with the image of someone with their pants down desperately trying to think of an excuse, 'to be caught rapid' is merely referring to being caught in the very act of wrongdoing, which only by chance may indeed see you with your pants down!

~ **Up Shit Creek without a paddle:** Yep, we have a Shit Creek in Ireland too.

~ **Found out:** While this can indicate the person has been caught doing something, if mentioned on the sports field it means that the opposition has your number and you are going to be in for a long game. A full-back's worst nightmare is to be 'found out' – the nippy full-forward will know that he can't cope with the low fast ball and he will be substituted long before the half-time whistle.

INSULTS

Irish people are not behind in coming forward and calling you a name, and we don't lack our fair share of insults, especially when you've annoyed or angered us.

TO APPLAUD YOUR SUCCESS, WE MIGHT SAY ...

I had one of those but the wheel came off.

TO COMPLIMENT YOUR APPEARANCE ...

You look like you've fallen from the ugly tree and hit every branch on the way down, with a face that would drive rats from a barn and a mouth on ya that would turn milk sour.

TO APPRECIATE YOUR GENEROSITY ...

You're as mean as ditch water, would peel an orange in your pocket and wouldn't give someone the steam off your piss.

TO TRUMPET YOUR TIME-KEEPING ...

You'd be late for your own funeral.

TO PRAISE YOUR ENDEAVOUR ...

If work was bed you'd sleep on the floor and you'd live in one ear and grow spuds out the other.

TO CELEBRATE YOUR INTELLIGENCE ...

You're as thick as shit but only half as useful, a ham sandwich short of a picnic, as helpful as tits on a bull and you don't know your arse from your elbow.

SOCIAL CUSTOMS

—

Social customs are the actions and behaviours that are expected of a particular culture. In Ireland we have plenty, and while it is handy to understand some of these, it is handier again to know what to call them.

GiViNG OUT

Getting annoyed over something or with someone is a national pastime in Ireland, which we dubiously call giving out. We have several other terms for this traditional endeavour.

Eat the head off someone: The kind of giving out you hear happening to someone else and makes you think 'Jaysus, I'm glad I'm not yer wan!'

Have a go at someone: While this can also mean physically hitting another person, by and large it refers to the practice of giving out to someone you don't really know, such as a politician. In such instances the substance of what is being said is less important than the tone of voice.

Give out shite: A favourite with teachers, particularly back in the early '90s when a student hadn't done their home-work, hadn't bothered to come up with an excuse, had forgotten their journal, or, worst of all, were smiling while they were being given out to.

Tore strips off him: Very common in junior GAA dressing rooms at halftime when the home team are losing against the local rivals and the full-back has just got himself sent off for back-chatting the ref.

Give out yards: This is very similar to giving out but it is what your mother does when she finds out that not only did you leave your bedroom in a complete mess, you forgot to take out the dog, water the plants, turn off the immersion and were watching TV when you should have been studying.

Pull someone up: While this phrase sounds like the type of sex scandal that would force a congressman from office, this is in fact the act of giving out to someone, often an employee, for a mistake.

Put someone in their place: This is the type of giving out that happens when a driver cuts off a fellow motorist only to find out he was an off-duty guard.

Tell off: Another innuendo-laden admonishment that is reserved for misdemeanours like pulling your golf trolley across the green or taking the kettle off the stove before it's fully boiled.

Get a bollicking: What happens to you on a building site when you forget to wash out the cement mixer at the end of the day.

NOTiONS

A danger that comes from a move to the city, buying a new car or winning the bingo is that the person affected starts to think they are better than other people. You know this is happening to someone when you overhear people (usually their family, neighbours or friends) saying the following.

HE'S FAiR BiG-HEADED: You think you're better than others due to the fact that you play full-forward, own an Audi or once shifted your one from that band they created on TV.

SHE'S STARTiNG TO HAVE NOTiONS: She's getting a statue put into the garden; only buys water sold in glass bottles; likes to order dinner in the language of the food; calls her son Sequoia or Acai or Cheyenne and pronounces scone 'scon'.

THiNK THEY'RE SOMEONE: While you would hope that everyone would 'think they're someone', this is actually a cutting observation that the person thinks they are someone better than everyone else.

HE'S BEGiNNiNG TO GET AHEAD OF HiMSELF: Scores a flukey goal and now thinks he should take the penalties, wins a mug on *Larry's Just-A-Minute* and thinks he might join Mensa, or doesn't burn the scrambled egg so decides to invite the family over for Sunday lunch.

HE'S ROSE ABOVE HIS STATION: Actually serving Communion when he was nothing more than a basket collector last Sunday.

TOO BIG FOR HIS BOOTS: If you hear this being said of someone it usually means the beginning of the end for many a coach, star player, politician or musician, as public opinion starts to turn against them.

A STEP ABOVE BUTTERMILK: Worse when said by someone of the older generation.

HE'S BIG WHEN HE'S OUT LIKE A DONKEY'S FLUTE: Signifying someone who likes to show off when out for the night – although to be frank, it's a little harsh on the donkey.

FULL OF THEMSELVES: While probably better than the slightly more cannibalistic 'full of someone else', this expression is another that suggests they are just too big for their boots.

THINKS ALL HER GEESE ARE SWANS: Has notions above her station, particularly concerning her children.

HELPiNG

Irish people love to help even if they might complain about it sometimes. This may come from the old Irish tradition of the meitheal, where people in rural communities helped each other in turn with farming work. Unsurprisingly, we have several words and phrases for helping each other.

Chip in: This is when you hear that someone needs a bit of a boost and everyone 'chips in a few quid' to help get them back on their feet. Fair play to ya.

Muck in: Where everyone gets their hands dirty to help someone out, sometimes literally.

Flahulach (Flaithiúlach): While occasionally employed for that person who is forever buying rounds at the bar for a middle-aged hen party from Essex he'll never meet again, 'flahulach' simply refers to someone who is generous with money and can always be counted on to help out a friend in need.

A dig out: Occasionally cash, but can just as easily refer to general help, a 'dig out' is when someone has encountered an unexpected setback smaller than bankruptcy and needs some immediate help. Generally speaking, it is best to 'offer a dig out' rather than wait for someone to ask for one.

GiViNG DiRECTiONS OR iNSTRUCTiONS

Another way Irish people like to help is by giving directions to those who find themselves a little lost, which can be as confusing as they are colourful.

> **Straight on left:** This means the road will veer off in that direction and you are to follow it.

> **No, the other right:** For when you misunderstand the instructions.

> **Go around the roundabout:** Just in case you thought of actually driving straight over it.

> **Take the next left, right?:** Huh?!

> **After about a half-mile you'll come across Dolan's pub where you'll meet a junction. There will be a road to the left. Don't take it:** Because we also like to give directions by telling people what road not to travel along.

LOOKiNG AT STUFF

Irish people generally do not like people staring at them. As a result, if you hear someone saying to you 'What are you staring at?' or 'Do you mind?' it might be due to an over-long look on your part. If this happens to you just apologise and look away. So instead of staring, there are several other ways Irish people observe daily life.

... **Goo:** Someone has collapsed around the corner and the emergency services are on the scene. This is ideal territory for having a 'quick goo' to see what's happening.

... **Rubber-necking:** The same except on the motorway and the reason why we now have a constant two-mile tail-back. If you 'rubber-neck' it is important to give out about all the rubber-neckers ahead of you causing the delay before you slow down yourself to have a look.

... **Glance:** The perfect type of quick look at someone you fancy. 'Glance over at him to see if he's looking over here'.

... **Juke:** What you tell your husband up North when you want to give the impression that you are not really clothes shopping, but are 'just having a quick juke to see if there is anything on special offer. I won't be five minutes.'

··· **Scan:** What people usually do when looking around a bar for someone or pretending to look for someone while really checking out the talent.

··· **Gander:** This is a good deal longer than a scan. It tends to be common amongst those who don't have the best eyesight and may need a little longer to figure out if they recognise anyone in a busy pub.

··· **Gleek:** Like a 'scan' up North.

APOLOGiSING

One social custom that visitors to Ireland can struggle with is how we seem to be constantly apologising. The thing is, we say 'sorry' a hell of a lot, but we don't always mean it, or at least not in the traditional sense. To help with this, it is useful to appreciate four of the very different ways we say sorry.

1. Genuinely sorry. This is when we say 'sorry' because we really did mess up. We were wrong. We were inconsiderate of your feelings. We made a mistake. And we want to own up and apologise for the genuine hurt, distress and sadness we may have caused. By and large that's not the sorry you'll hear us say.

How to identify this 'sorry': You will be expecting it because the person has just cheated on you, reversed over your dog or accidentally set fire to your house. The person saying it will also look genuinely upset and may even be crying.

2. 'Sorry' because we are in your way. A distant relation to the first, we are still in the wrong, but it's no big deal. For instance, we might have bumped into you because we weren't watching where we were going, forgot to offer you a cup of tea or forgot to record *Game of Thrones* for you. For these 'sorrys', while we might genuinely feel bad for our actions, we are not that sorry that a trip to the confessional will be needed.

How to identify this 'sorry': The person will often be looking down towards the ground, grimacing or rubbing their brow as they try to figure out how they made the mistake in the first place. If you say 'don't worry about it', the person will usually respond by immediately offering to make up for it, often by buying you a drink.

3. 'Sorry' because you are in our way. Understandably difficult for non-Irish people, this is the 'sorry' said when it is **you** who bumped into us, who forced us to get out of **your** way, or **you** who forgot to bring out the tea we ordered – we are saying sorry to remind **you**. In such cases, we are absolutely 'not sorry' but are subconsciously putting the words into your mouth. While it can be nice for you to acknowledge your mistake, what absolutely does not work is telling us that it is all right, that we should not worry about it or, worse yet, forgive us for our trespasses.

How to identify this 'sorry': Ask yourself a question – do you think we have something to be genuinely sorry for? If you don't think we do, then it is you who has probably screwed up.

4. 'Sorry' because we are looking for the way. The final 'sorry' is for when we want to get your attention. Though not as tricky as others, it can be a little confusing. This 'sorry' is what we use when asking for directions, looking to give an order or want to call attention to something. Again, we are not sorry, we are just politely interrupting.

How to identify this 'sorry': We will be wearing a polite smile, may even have a little hand up and will always follow it with a question.

NUDiTY

Despite the weather, people in Ireland do like to get naked. Just check out the local GAA communal showers, our annual day of summer and the ancient Irish practice of mooning, where someone was actually employed to drop their drawers at a Gaelic feast. Unsurprisingly, then, we have multiple words and phrases for being absolutely 'clothless'.

In the nip: This is generally reserved for when you are caught naked by mistake. Common occurrences are when you forget the 'do not disturb' on your hotel room or are met by a houseguest when you tip-toe downstairs late at night for a glass of water.

Starkers: The state of undress associated with those running into the sea around Christmas just for the craic.

Belly-naked: National pastime that breaks out around 12 May (or thereabouts) every year when we get the first blast of warm sunshine. Belly-naked usually means that person still has their bottoms on.

Bollick-naked: The grown-up cousin of belly-naked and often only used when the listener refuses to believe that the person being talked about actually streaked across the Intermediate County Hurling Semi-Final as a protest against declining meat prices. 'When you said Michael ran across the field without any clothes on, you mean like, just wearing shorts?' 'No, I mean he was bollick-naked!'

TALKiNG

Though we do like to pride ourselves on our storytelling, as a nation we are occasionally prone to overdoing it. There are multiple ways this can happen.

RABBiTiNG ON: The type of monologue that characterises first-date disasters when one side just won't shut up due to the nerves.

GUFF: Pure nonsense without any evidence and often tainted by some sort of prejudice.

THE SAME OL' SPiEL: Very like guff but is actually the nonsense repeated almost word for word and trotted out every time a particular issue comes up.

SHiTE TALK: This is the end-of-night conversation that takes place in the local when everyone with sense has gone home.

BLATHERiNG: Common in older members of the extended family who just go on and on and on giving advice and life lessons that no one asked for.

RÁIMÉIS: A general opinion on a matter, often politics, that is complete and utter rubbish.

TALKING A LOAD OF BOLLIX: Kind of like the above but involving a whole catalogue of statements that are ráiméis.

WAFFLING: Sounds full of substance but is completely full of shite.

HARPING ON: It sounded grand to begin with, but 10 minutes later and they are still 'harping on'.

TOILETING

It is not uncommon for Irish people to notify each other when they are going to the bathroom. Why this is the case, no one quite knows. However, what we do know is that no one likes to repeat that they are going to the bathroom, so it can be helpful for visitors to know what the person you're drinking with has said when they suddenly disappear. The first set of terms indicates the person is going to the toilet in the first place.

Going to the jacks: While jacks mean the bathroom, the word is mainly associated with pub and club toilets.

Off to the bog: Male-oriented and refers mainly to the fact they are going to use a cubicle over a urinal.

Leithreas: What we called it when we were in school and wanted permission to go outside to use it when it was actually inside. Long story.

THE NEXT ARE FOR NUMBER ONES:

● **Pee:** Strange thing to say, if the person is older than 10.

● **Piss:** Obvious one here, especially on a night out.

- **Whizz:** This is an outdoorsy type of urination but one done in town, usually in someone's bushes or around the corner from the takeaway. It is undertaken very speedily so as not to get caught.

- **Slash:** Commonly spotted on the lay-bys beside motorways.

- **Jimmy riddle:** English import that gives no indication as to how the person is actually urinating.

- **Leak:** This is a type of toilet trip that you've been holding in, hence the person telling you that they 'need' to take a leak, otherwise that's exactly what they are going to spring.

- **Shake hands with the best man:** If your date ever says this to you, don't even finish your drink. Time to leave.

AND THE FINAL ARE FOR NUMBER TWOS, OTHER THAN THE OBVIOUS ONES BEGINNING WITH 'SH'.

- **A dump:** Doesn't really need further explaining.

- **Posting a letter:** Sometimes needs further explaining, especially when the person doesn't have a letter.

SLAGGING

Few countries turn insulting each other into as much of an art form as Ireland. Here are some of our nice ways to insult someone.

Slagging: Perhaps our most cherished way of insulting someone, 'slagging' is that good-natured ribbing that occurs between friends and family. While it might sound somewhat serious to the outside ear, the person you're calling 'some bollix' or a 'cute hoor' knows you are only joking, and that no matter how many times you 'slag off' their likes, loves, pastimes or personality you really do hold them in great affection.

Taking the mick: Often associated with an older brother who goes through the whole back album of your failed romances during your stag party.

Taking the piss: While this can mean someone taking complete advantage of a kind offer (like when you tell your friend to crash as long as they like and they end up staying through the winter), 'taking the piss' usually means to slag someone off in a genial way by having a laugh at their new car, haircut, jumper etc.

Rip the piss: Like 'taking the piss', except when everyone joins in to slag the friend off up until the point he is about to go home. Only then do you stop (if only for a while).

Lambasted: The type of slagging a bloke would get if he let slip that his favourite programme was *Strictly Come Dancing*, he couldn't make it out for a pint due to his Pilates class or because he used the word 'sequins'. All good-natured.

HOWEVER, WE ALSO HAVE A FEW NOT-NICE WAYS TO INSULT SOMEONE.

Have a dig at: The interesting thing about 'having a dig at someone' is that they don't even have to be present, and normally aren't!

Sledging: This insulting takes place on the football field and includes remarking upon the appearance of your opposite number or commenting on the parentage of the person you've been tasked with marking.

SWEARING

In Ireland, we tend to swear a good deal. So much so that few people bat an eyelid if they hear our favourite sailor's oath said on television (often by winning captains of football teams who then immediately apologise, usually to Marty). That said, despite the F-word never being more popular in the country, freelancing as a noun, adjective, verb, preposition, conjunction, adverb, pronoun and indefinite article, its use by anyone under the age of 18 is still roundly frowned upon. Indeed, most 13-year-olds worth their salt would know that not until they were living under someone else's roof would they be allowed utter it with gleeful abandon. As a result, a plethora of would-be F-word saccharin substitutes have been developed.

⚡ **Sugar:** This is what we begin with when we are younger. Sugar is sweet and so are we, even if we are shouting the word at the top of our voices. Employed mostly for when our toys break down or the batteries run out.

⚡ **Flip:** A fun-loving type of F-word that we generally use when things aren't that bad, like colouring outside the lines, failing to score a basket or spilling a bit of tea as we were bringing it over to our parents.

⚡ **Fizz it:** This is an exceptionally endearing version of the F-word popular amongst older farmers.

⚡ **Hump it:** As above, but angrier, although they do have the option of saying 'fizz it to hell' which is as angry as 'hump it'.

⚡ **Frig:** Common one, especially for when you are trying to fix something but have only gone and made it worse.

⚡ **Feck:** Not harsh enough for parents to chastise their children, feck was coarse enough that it gave the utterer a taste of its troublemaking older brother. Feck would ultimately become the 'gateway' curse, with anyone who used 'feck' inevitably moving on to harder curses by the time they were 16 or 17.

⚡ **Shite:** Not to be confused with the principal character in a Japanese Noh play, the word 'shite', while often referring to a type of faecal matter, is also used extensively across Ireland to articulate disgust. To best understand the context, it is important to first identify the word that precedes it.

⚡ **Complete shite:** Used to describe a work of art (movie, TV programme, album, supposed piece etc.) that is dreadful from start to finish.

- ⚡ **Utter shite:** More specific to a performance, particularly of a sporting nature that ends in a team losing badly.

- ⚡ **Pure shite:** This is handy when it is something of yours you are describing, like the exam you've just completed or the night out you just had.

- ⚡ **Wee shite:** Describes a young person, usually a male relation, who has upset you because they've used up all your deodorant, told your parents about your plans to sneak out or taken the front seat of the car on the way to mass.

- ⚡ **Go and shite:** This is best employed when someone is slagging you off and you haven't any comeback.

CURSES

Aside from the wide variety of modern ways to tell someone to eff-off, Ireland has a rich history of traditional curses. These past profanities had a much deeper level of thought put into them, truly reflecting the fact you were angry with the person you were using them on. Here are some classics and who best to direct them to.

May your kettle never boil: Particularly harsh, for mothers, aunts and grannies.

May your milk never churn: Aimed more at dairy farmers than at new mothers.

May you be afflicted with an itch but not have the nails to scratch it: Popular before the advent of power showers and long-handled back scrubs.

May your wood always be knotted: While you might leave it up to the 'cursee' as to how they'd like to interpret this, generally speaking it refers to cutting timber for firewood.

May your children promise much but offer nothing: Directed specifically at old busybodies in the village who do nothing but gossip about you.

May you get the runs on your wedding night: Commonly levelled at a man who ran off with your girlfriend or at least hooked up with someone you fancied before you had a chance to.

May you always be a widow: The more robust female equivalent to the above.

May you melt off the earth like snow off a ditch: To be used only for those people who've wronged you in the worst possible ways – don't be saying this to your younger brother for breaking the tea-stand you made in woodwork class.

May the cat eat you and may the divil eat the cat: A proper curse, especially for feline-lovers.

While each of these jinxes will suffice, perhaps the grand-daddy of old oaths is the following.

May those who love us love us,
And those that don't love us,
May God turn their hearts.
And if he doesn't turn their hearts,
May he turn their ankles,
So we'll know them by their limping.

Harsh.

Though these curses may no longer as widely used, it doesn't stop you from making up your own. Yes, you might sound a little different but there's nothing like a good old-fashioned make-it-uppee to get things off your chest.

May you turn up at a Ryanair check-in without your boarding pass.

May your Celebration box be full of Bountys and empty wrappers.

May you be seated next to your ex at your next wedding.

May all your Christmas presents be socks.

May you forget the fantasy football deadline.

May you accidentally post a nudie photo on your Facebook profile.

May you always receive that hospital pass.

May the red sock be found in your washing.

May you be caught doing 56 km/h in a 50 km/h zone.

May you never really find out where the smell is coming from.

BLESSINGS

While they have become less and less common in daily usage, the Irish do have a whole slew of traditional blessings to draw from, particularly upon someone's departure. To help understand exactly (or not) what they mean, we've gone to the effort of including a modern interpretation with each.

MAY THE ROAD RISE TO MEET YOU:
May the way home be well signposted with cats' eyes to keep you between the lines.

MAY THE WIND ALWAYS BE AT YOUR BACK:
At the interval when you're only a point ahead, may the wind turn and give you a further advantage in the second half.

MAY THE WALLS OF YOUR HOME NEVER FALL IN AND THOSE WITHIN THEM NEVER FALL OUT:
May the house you bought not be affected by pyrite and may everyone take their turn to do the dishes.

MAY THE SADDEST DAY OF YOUR FUTURE BE NO WORSE THAN THE HAPPIEST DAY OF YOUR PAST:

May your becoming redundant next year be as much craic as your wedding last July.

MAY THE FROST NEVER AFFLICT YOUR SPUDS:

May the results come back negative.

MAY THE DUST OF YOUR CARRIAGE BLIND THE EYES OF YOUR FOES:

May road chippings thrown up by your car hit that old fecker who objected to your planning permission.

MAY THE RAINS SWEEP GENTLE ACROSS YOUR FIELDS:

May the flooding not affect your café.

MAY THE ENEMIES OF IRELAND NEVER MEET A FRIEND:

England and penalty kicks. Enough said.

MAY YOU LIVE FOR A HUNDRED YEARS WITH ONE EXTRA YEAR TO REPENT:

May you live for at least a hundred years and in the final year turn yourself in for that diesel-laundering racket that funded your retirement.

AS YOU SLIDE DOWN THE BANNISTER OF LIFE, MAY THE SPLINTERS NEVER POINT IN THE WRONG DIRECTION:

As you go through life, may you never get caught speeding, buy an apartment at the height of the boom, fail to get that promotion or find your wife in bed with the milkman.

MAY YOU LIVE AS LONG AS YOU WANT, AND NEVER WANT AS LONG AS YOU LIVE:

May you get to retire to the Caribbean with a great big court settlement.

MAY THE SUN SHINE SOFT ON YOUR FIELD:

May it not be raining during your wedding photos.

MAY YOU BE IN HEAVEN A HALF-HOUR BEFORE THE DEVIL KNOWS YOU'RE GONE:

May you be dead before Revenue finds out you owe them €143,000 in back taxes

SPECIAL OCCASIONS

In Ireland, there are many special occasions that we mark, enjoy and welcome. Some of these will be very familiar to visitors, such as Christmas, Christenings, Easter, weddings, Halloween and Bank Holidays, while some of them will be not so familiar, either due to the name or the event. Here are a few that can prove a little curious:

- **St Patrick's Day/Paddy's Day:** Our national day. Under no circumstances – on pain of death – do you call it Patty's Day.

- **Communions and Confirmations:** Quasi-religious celebrations that allow families to get all dressed up and have a big meal together while their kids count their earnings. What?! It's proper religious?!

- **The Debs:** See that stretch Hummer driving between Athboy and Navan? Those teenagers dressed up like it's a wedding outside the local with their parents taking their photos on a Wednesday? Drive by a dozen bedraggled youngsters in tuxes and gowns on your way to work at 6am? That's the Debs. The Debs, or Debutantes Ball, is the Irish equivalent of prom night, when ex-Leaving Cert students honour their time in school by socialising, celebrating and drinking way too many Jägerbombs.

> **Holliers:** Not an actual day, but an event when the nation gets sick of the lack of sun and heads off to Costa del Spain for a fortnight.

> **The Big Day:** Everyone knows what the big day is in Ireland. It is the day when you invite your friends, family and aunts and uncles you haven't seen since Christmas of '92. It's also called your wedding.

> **December the 8th:** On this day, in the era before online retail outlets, half the country used to come up to the city and go shopping.

> **St Stephen's Day:** This is what Irish people call the day after Christmas Day, which the British call Boxing Day. This is a day when we celebrate pubs re-opening, strange men with blackened faces calling to your door to sing badly, turkey leftovers and some type of sport that involves gambling.

MASS

Part leisure, part special occasion, part the worst 45 minutes children spent in the company of their parents, mass was part and parcel of traditional Irish life growing up. While mass and praying usually took place in a church, one of which was in almost every town and village in Ireland, there was a period of time in Irish history where mass could happen anywhere and at any time. There are a few terms related to it that are worth knowing.

NOVENA: Kind of like the holy Olympics in that this mass goes on over a couple of weeks with huge crowds, loads of merchandise and competitors from Africa (i.e. the missionaries) who are always the most successful.

THE HOLY DIP: The big container of holy water located at the entrance to a church.

CEMETERY SUNDAYS: A Sunday in the summer when the relatives of the dead meet in a graveyard to exchange stories, remember loved ones, be eaten by midges and say the Rosary.

THE ROSARY: Generally involved 50 'Hail Marys' led by someone quite elderly and finished by the assembly. Ten 'Hail Marys' is often referred to as a 'decade of the Rosary'. The term decade is an apt term, especially when the person leading is very, very old, speaks quite slowly and loses track of the amount of 'Hail Marys' they have already called. Children can be observed physically growing up during Cemetery Sundays when this occurs.

RELICS: An actual primary source of history (usually a piece of the real Crucifix, no word of a lie) that the most reverent aunt in the extended family held on to. Locked and hidden away somewhere in the front room, and only comes out during house masses.

THE CRYING ROOM: Aren't baby children beautiful? Yes, they are, but in churches there is only one place for them and that is the crying room. Here, sound-proofing that would make a Pink Floyd tribute act proud keeps in their noise. But aren't they beautiful all the same?

IRiSH GRAMMAR

—

What most characterises how we speak English is probably the fact that we once spoke Irish, or Gaeilge. And while Gaeilge has contributed many a fine word to the English language, it is most famous for how it has coloured many of the words and phrases that do come out of our mouths.

WORDS IRELAND GAVE TO THE WORLD

While Ireland has generally taken the English language and coloured it to fit us, it has also given back. In fact, in English today there are a few dozen words in common usage that come from Ireland – or at least that we claim come from Ireland. If we were to pick a team, here would be our first fifteen.

Slogan: From sluagh-ghairm meaning battle-shout, this was first used all the way back in the early 18th century by Gaelic clans about to battle (and generally lose) against their English counterparts.

Kybosh: While there exist a few schools of thought on its origin, from Yiddish to Turkish, one belief is that 'kybosh', meaning 'to put an end to', comes from 'an chaip bháis' or 'the cap of death'. This was the black cap worn by a judge when passing a sentence of capital punishment.

Smithereens: Derived from the Irish smidiríní, which means 'little bits'. 'To smash to smithereens' is exactly what full-backs try to do to their opposite numbers.

Dig: This dig is neither the dig you do in the garden nor the dig you do into the stomach of an opponent by way of an introduction. Instead, it is the 'dig' that you do in the Bronx, New York, as in 'You dig?'. This is rumoured to have come from little old Irish nuns who did missionary work in the Caribbean. Working with and alongside Afro-Caribbeans, they would often ask the question 'An dtuigeann tú?' as Gaeilge, which means 'Do you understand?' With a silent 't', 'dtuigeann tú' shortened and migrated northwards to eventually find its way into African-American neighbour-hoods and '70s Blaxploitation movies.

Gob: The Irish for 'beak', this has increasingly become a slang word for mouth, as in to get sent off for 'opening your gob to the referee'.

Bog: From 'bogach', meaning marsh or peatland, which is that difficult terrain common to Irish midlands.

Phoney: This all started in Britain in the 19th century, when tricksters would make a great show of 'finding' a gold ring, which they would then sell to a passer-by. Unfortunately for the passer-by, the gold ring was usually brass. And because the swindler was usually Irish, the Irish word for ring – 'fáinne' – lent its name to the trick that became known as the 'fawney rig'. When the trick emigrated westwards to the US, 'fawney' became 'phoney', and the word stuck. The word became legendary when Holden Caulfield used it more than forty times in the *Catcher in the Rye*, though thankfully never because he was swindled into buying a brass ring from an Irish trickster.

Whiskey: Though the Scots might disagree, whiskey comes from the Anglicisation of the Irish word for it – 'uisce beatha' – literally meaning the 'water of life'. Do we really need to say more?

Shebeen: This unlicensed place to sell alcohol originates in the Gaelic word 'síbín', meaning mugful, which is exactly what you would have got when you slipped into such an establishment way back when.

Cross: Not the cross of a ball towards the goal, but the 'cross' of Christian fame. While the original source of the word is the Latin 'crux', there are a few theories that suggest the English word didn't come directly from it but indirectly through the Irish word for 'crux', which was 'cros'.

Clock: A real old one here. Irish missionaries to Europe brought 'hand-bells', and the Irish for bell is 'clog', which the Old German language translated into 'glocka', which in modern German became 'glocke', which would eventually arrive in English via Flemish to symbolise the 'clock'.

Craic: Started life in England as 'crack', meaning fun and enjoyment, before the Ulster Scots brought it to Ireland. However, presumably because the Irish felt they weren't using the word correctly, we took it over, turned it into 'craic' and then sold it back to the English.

Slew: Meaning a lot, as in he had a 'slew of chances in front of the goal'. This word comes from the Irish 'sluagh', meaning 'a large number of'.

Galore: Another great Irish one here that was made famous by James Bond's love interest Pussy Galore. 'Galore' comes from the Irish 'go leor', meaning 'until plenty'.

Spondulicks: While some say that 'spondulicks' comes from the Greek shell the 'spondylos', which was used for currency, a less probable but certainly more colourful origin of this word is from the Irish 'sponc', meaning sperm and 'diúlaigh' meaning 'from the fellow' (as if it came from any-where else!?). The idea was that producing sperm was like making money. Go figure!

PHRASAL VERBS

Phrasal who? These are the types of phrases that mix a verb and an adjective or preposition to make something new. They are common throughout the English language – 'bring in', 'put through', 'carry away', 'break down', 'throw up' – but in Ireland we use a few of our own as well.

- **Pass out:** People can 'pass out' due to drink or exhaustion, but in Ireland we prefer to pass out while driving. While this might scare the bejaysus out of a visiting passenger, it simply means to overtake another car while still conscious.

- **Let on:** Sounds like being allowed onto a bus, but actually means to pretend in the way you might 'let on' to be 'ill' the day after your local team won the county final.

- **Give out:** While this refers to an Irish national hobby, 'giving out' to the unaware can sound like some sort of sexual favour. It's not. It's just your mother scolding you for leaving your bedroom in a complete mess.

- **Let off:** Can mean to make 500 people redundant, but in Ireland it is more likely a euphemism for farting and the reason everyone in the room is now covering their noses.

- **Go hard on:** If someone comes home from work saying that the boss 'has gone hard on them', don't worry – it's not a lawsuit in the making, it's just that the boss has been quite tough and demanding.

CRAIC AND OTHER WORDS THAT SOUND SUSPICIOUSLY LIKE DRUGS

CRAIC (PRONOUNCED 'CRACK'): At this stage in Irish history, every US immigration official is probably aware that an Irish visitor looking for 'fierce craic', 'savage craic', 'mighty craic' or 'some craic' is simply hoping to have a good night on the beer.

DOPE: Neither marijuana nor heroin but the type of individual who during the Boom used to earn €50 an hour driving a three-tonne dumper around a building site with the handbrake on.

WIRED: Particularly common amongst six-year-olds who have just drunk their mother's coffee while she was on the phone. This term does not mean on drugs but simply refers to someone whose state of mind is acting much more frenetically than can be good for you.

HIGH AS A KITE: Again, not high on drugs, but refers to someone whose enthusiasm has gotten the better of them. Think an eight-year-old on Christmas Eve.

HASH: While this might be referring to cannabis, it is just as likely the person is referring to an utter mess, i.e. 'the hash they made' of an exam, a driving test or a relationship due to the misreading of a question, a stop sign or a sartorial query.

THIRTY-THREE

Of the myriad things that can give an Irish person abroad away – red hair, bad teeth, pale skin and wearing the county jersey – perhaps one of the strongest is how we say the number 33. Why it is that we seem genetically incapable of pronouncing 'th' correctly is open to debate, but one theory (pronounced 'teary') is that 'th' didn't exist as Gaeilge, so when the English started importing the language into Ireland, the locals didn't have the linguistic tools to master the 'th', something that continues to this day. And that is why many of us continue to struggle with words such as the below.

- The
- Thirty-three and a third
- Thoroughly
- Thick
- Thin
- Thorny
- Thumb
- Theatre
- Theory
- Thanks

THE

Despite having difficulty pronouncing it, Irish people have no problem putting 'the' in front of things it has absolutely no place beside, particularly in the case of more recent arrivals to Ireland.

THE FACEBOOK
THE GOOGLE
THE YOUTUBE
THE SKYPE
THE TWITTER

Of course, we don't just mess up the names of things by adding a 'the'. When we can't possibly get away with this, we do our best to put an 's' at the end – something we are particularly fond of doing to supermarkets.

TESCOS
LIDLS
ALDIS
SUPERVALUS

OTHER WORDS WE CAN'T PRONOUNCE

Along with the 'th' family, there is a whole host of other words we can't pronounce, not because of anything technically complex about them, but rather because a) we were never told how to pronounce them correctly in the first place, or b) no one else knows we are pronouncing them wrong.

Nuptial: The fancy way we now talk about our weddings even if they still involve beef or salmon, Sweet Caroline and a drunken uncle.

Should be pronounced: Nup-shul. How we actually pronounce it: Nup-choo-al.

Bruschetta: That classic Italian appetiser we rarely get when there's also spicy chickens wings on the menu.

Should be pronounced: 'Bru-sket-ah'. How we actually pronounce it: 'bru-shett-ah.

Haute Couture: Kind of like Penneys but not.

Should be pronounced: 'oat cu-tu-r'. How we actually pronounce it: 'haw-tee cow-chur'.

Tenterhooks: What we can feel on if we are in a state of tension or uncertainty.

Should be pronounced: 'tenter-hooks', because it has a 't' like! How we actually pronounce it: 'tender-hooks'.

Committee: The life-blood of any local GAA club.

Should be pronounced: 'kuh-mit-tee'. How we actually pronounce it: 'commm-mit-ee'.

Film: Like a movie.

Should be pronounced: 'filmmmm', with the 'm' drifting off like an expensive perfume. How we actually pronounce it: 'fill-um'.

Mischievous: What some of the best cat videos online are all about.

Should be pronounced: 'mis-chuv-us'. How we actually pronounce it: 'mis-cheev-ee-us'.

Asterisk: The small dot-type figure used at the end of a word to denote an additional meaning written below.

Should be pronounced: 'as-ter-isk'. How we actually pronounce it: 'ast-er-ix', like that little moustachioed Gaul who used to put it up to the Romans.

Et cetera: Meaning all those other items on a list you couldn't be bothered to write down.

Should be pronounced: 'et-cet-er-ah'. How we actually pronounce it: 'ex-cet-er-ah'.

Quinoa: That hipster superfood that only a few people know how to cook properly.

Should be pronounced: 'keen-wah'. How we actually pronounce it: 'kin-oh-ah'/ 'quinn-oh-ah'/ 'queue-in-oh-ah'.

Sudoku: The thinking man's simplex crossword.

Should be pronounced: 'soo-doh-coo'. How we actually pronounce it: 'suh-doh-cu'.

Along with these, there are some words that we know how to pronounce, but still can't quite get the hang of.

Vehicle: As in a moving vehicle.

Should be pronounced: 'vee-hick-ul'. How we actually pronounce it: 'veh-ick-ul'.

Remember: I don't need to tell you what remember means.

Should be pronounced: er... 're-mem-ber'. How we actually pronounce it: 'mem-ber', as if you failed to member the 're' part.

Specific: Meaning exact.

Should be pronounced: 'spec-if-ic'. How we actually pronounce it: 'pac-if-ic', like the Atlantic except bigger.

MORE WORDS IRELAND GAVE TO THE WORLD

The second set of words and phrases that Ireland gave to the English language – whether they wanted them or not – originate in Irish places.

DONNYBROOK, COUNTY DUBLIN: Donnybrook is more synonymous today with the home of the national broadcaster, RTÉ, and the place where half of Ireland used to send in postcards to *The Late Late Show* hoping to win a holiday to Florida and £1,000 spending money. However, from at least the 13th century until the middle of the 1800s, it was home to a week-long fair that by Friday was a cross between a féile and a prison riot. So crazy did it become that this now upmarket and expensive suburb once lent its name to a 'a scene of uproar and disorder'.

BALLYHOOLY, COUNTY CORK: Never to be outdone by its arch-rival Dublin, Cork is also responsible for a description of 'utter pandemonium' with the small village of 'Ballyhooly' also entering the English language. Though today Ballyhooly is a quaint little village in north Cork that, according to Wikipedia, is home to several pubs, a church, a community centre and a petrol station with a shop (because you can't forget the shop), back in the early 1800s it became notorious for faction fighting. Faction fighting was a mass brawl that could involve hundreds and even thousands of antagonists kicking the shite out of each other. This faction fighting (not to mixed up with fraction fighting, where thirds, quarters and eighths go at it) was an Irish phenomenon that was usually based on families or parishes. With little rhyme or reason to the fights except that there was nothing much on the TV back then, the brawls would often result in the deaths of at least one participant and the maiming and injuring of scores more. While they were concentrated in the province of Munster, Ballyhooly became particularly synonymous with these type of fights, with at least one infamous 1819 brawl actually beginning in the local church.

LIMERICK, COUNTY LIMERICK: Why or how the strict five-line AABBA rhyming scheme known as a 'limerick' came from here is somewhat uncertain, though it might come from the 18th-century Maigue Poets who hailed from the county.

What is more certain is that while some examples of limericks can be amusing, you certainly wouldn't base a night's entertainment around them.

BANAGHER, COUNTY OFFALY: The final place of note is the small town of Banagher in west Offaly that can be heard in the phrase 'That beats Banagher!', a familiar response to something extraordinary or absurd. The origin of this idiom is due to the fact that back in the day the place was a 'pocket borough' and, as such, the local lord got to nominate its representatives in parliament. This bizarrely undemocratic way of doing politics led to the saying coming into its own.

PRESENTLY PERFECT

Another way the Irish can come across as fierce lazy is down to how we sometimes use the word 'have' and the present perfect. Like most grammatical rules, we didn't learn it properly in school, but the present perfect is a tense that is used for unfinished or finished actions. It is created by using 'have' directly followed by a verb in the past tense. Examples include the following.

- I have baked the cake.

- I have done my homework.

- I have read the book.

- I have mowed the garden.

- I have fed the cat.

However, in Ireland, due to a long-running dispute between 'have' and verbs in the past tense (rumoured to be the result of a love triangle involving a relative clause), Irish people regularly avoid putting the two together, much in the same way we separate warring uncles at a family wedding. As a result, the end product is a sentence that sounds like the person speaking didn't carry out the work at all but instead got someone else to do it for them.

Consequently, 'I have baked the cake', becomes 'I have the cake baked', which makes the grammatically correct English speaker think, 'That's lovely, but by whom?'

❧ I have the homework done ... by a horde of first-year students I pay less than minimum wage?

❧ I have the book read ... to me by my 74-year-old mother?

❧ I have the garden mowed ... by a group of illegals that Trump wants to deport?

❧ I have the cat fed ... to a pack of ravenous crocodiles?

NOT ASKING FOR SOMETHING

Even more confusing for the grammatically correct English speaker is how we Irish don't like to ask for something when we are asking for something. Whether it is due to our desire to look after ourselves, down to our pride or just yet another influence of our native tongue, Irish people will regularly ask for your help by not asking for it.

For example, when we ask **'You can't pass the sugar there, can you'**, we want the sugar.

When we wonder if **'You couldn't change the channel over to the news, would ya'**, we want to watch the news.

When we inquire if **'You'll hardly give us a lift to the next town'**, we'd like you to give us a lift to the next town.

'You wouldn't lend us your lawnmower for an hour' means we want your lawnmower.

'**You couldn't throw us back in the football from your garden**' means we want our football back.

'**It's not possible you could ring us back later**' means we want you to ring us back later.

While '**There's no chance of the shift, is there**' means we want you to kiss us, we really want to kiss you.

EVEN MORE WORDS IRELAND GAVE TO THE WORLD

The third and final set of words and phrases that Ireland blessed the world with are those that derive from names of families living in or closely associated with Ireland – and what a fine group they are.

THE HOULIHANS FROM COUNTY LIMERICK: The first family to have offered their name for usage were the O'Houlihans (Hoolohans, Ó hUallacháins). In this obscure tale, it is said that they originated from Limerick before moving over the water to London where they lived at the end of the 19th century. If the Houlihans existed today, not only would they have brought down house prices in their surrounding estate, they would have also been stars of their own TV reality series. The reason for this was the outrageous and unruly behaviour for which they became infamous. It was to this type of behaviour that they would lend their name, so that others who followed similar conduct would become known as **hooligans.**

THE BOYCOTTS FROM COUNTY MAYO: While our second family, the Boycotts, may well have been an entirely lovely family who never cheated at bridge, kept their elbows off the table while they ate and sang songs on the way to church, this would all count for naught when Captain Charles Cunningham Boycott (Chucky to his friends, of which he would soon have none) decided to start evicting tenants from his land in Mayo. Having served first in the British military, a colonial army not known for their PR skills, Boycott became a land agent in the Lough Mask area of Mayo. However, when he decided to evict tenants who weren't keeping up with their payments, the community decided to socially ostracise him. People didn't greet him or his family in town, seasonal workers didn't turn up for his harvest and absolutely no one attended his bridge nights. It continued until he could no longer take it, so he packed his trunk and he and his family left for England. But not before he left his surname behind to become the practice of isolating someone or something – to **boycott**.

THE BALUBAS FROM COUNTY DEMOCRATIC REPUBLIC OF CONGO: Last but not least are the Balubas. Of course, not only are the Balubas not actually from the island of Ireland, they are not a family at all but are instead a tribe from the provinces of Kasai and Katanga in the south of the DR Congo. How their name became 'balooba' and entered the

English dictionary was down to their fatal ambush of a battalion of Irish peacekeepers in 1960. Due to this attack on a group of soldiers who were there to protect them, balooba became synonymous with someone who is crazy and untrustworthy, **'a right balooba, so he is'**, as well as being so drunk you cannot make any sense, **'he was absolutely balooba-ed'**.

AWFUL

'Awful' as an adjective is generally used in two ways. The first means something that is very bad or unpleasant, like an 'awful smell' or an 'awful mess' or an 'awful creep'. The second is used to emphasise the extent of something, especially something unpleasant, such as the time you made a move on your boss at a party and then realised that 'you've made an awful eejit of yourself'.

In Ireland, however, we have a third way. We also employ 'awful' to emphasise those things that are not 'awful' at all but are usually the opposite!

— **She is awful beautiful:** She looks gorgeous.

— **He's awful friendly:** He was very quick to buy a round for everyone.

— **They're awfully good:** They were really nice in letting everyone stay the night at such short notice.

— **It was awful craic:** You hadn't expected to stay out until midnight but it was so much fun there was no way you were going home early.

WORDS AND PHRASES WE DON'T REALLY USE

As in the animal kingdom, not all words or phrases survive in Ireland. Either due to the encroachment of man or natural selection, some words and phrases simply die off and become almost entirely extinct. Indeed, such words are no longer found in the wild and can only now be heard in zoos, nature reserves and badly scripted American crime dramas.

CÉAD MÍLE FÁILTE: Translating into English as 'a hundred thousand welcomes', this hasn't been heard outside of speeches welcoming foreign dignitaries for more than 20 years.

ERIN GO BRAGH: Though 'Erin go bragh', meaning 'Ireland forever', is no longer used outside of the cheap Irish souvenir mug market, it was once a common shout of Irish allegiance, particularly amongst the Irish diaspora. As well as being an emotive battle cry, it was also a famous slogan used on early pre-tricolour Irish flags, such as the one Wicklow man and Olympic long-jump silver medallist Peter O'Connor unfurled to replace the Union Jack back in 1906. With the help of his fellow Irish and Irish-American athletes who fended off security, Peter climbed up the pole at the Athens Olympic medal ceremony and proudly hung a green flag, complete with harp and 'Erin go bragh', which was the first time an Irish flag was used at an international event.

BEJAYPERS: Extinct distant relation to 'bejaysus'. The last person recorded using 'bejaypers' died during the '80s, having fallen through the frozen canal a mile outside of Longford town.

BEGORRAH: This term used to be employed to exclaim surprise and was thought to be a euphemistic substitute for 'by God' – 'Well begorrah your honour, I was not within a hundred yards of the pub when the fight broke out. I swear on my dead mother's life.' For more than 60 years, 'begorrah' was mandatory in any Hollywood script set in Ireland until someone told them that the last time it was heard was when we lived in black and white.

PÓG MO THÓIN: While, yes, this does mean kiss my arse, and yes, there are several times we would like someone to do it, this is simply not an expression we use and certainly not one we'd ever wear on a T-shirt.

BLARNEY: While the word still means 'speaking a load of crap', 'blarney' has gone the way of the VCR. That said, you can still go to Blarney Castle where the word originated. Here, you can be hung upside down by a strange man wearing gloves, kiss the Blarney Stone and receive the 'gift of the gab'; a phrase that means the ability to speak with eloquence and persuasion and also a phrase isn't used outside the grounds of Blarney Castle.

TOP O' THE MORNING TO YOU: This is what people would say to you if *The Truman Show* was recreated somewhere in east Galway. However, it was created in Seagrove Beach, Florida, where they said 'good morning, good afternoon, good evening and good night'. As a result, the only people who say 'top o' the morning to you' are those who are looking to get a box across the ears.

ME TRUSTED SHILLELAGH: Unless you are a multi-millionaire dance phenomenon who knows his way around a boxing ring, never use this.

YOUS, YE AND YIZ

In the Queen's English, the word 'you' can stand for one person or several. So when a teacher says 'Did you lift my car and hide it behind the gym?' he or she could be referring to one super-human pupil or the whole class.

In Irish or as Gaeilge we have two words for 'you': 'tú' for singular and 'sibh' for plural. It is not so surprising then, that when English came to Ireland we decided that one 'you' wasn't enough – so we also brought in yous, yiz and ye. While there seems to be little in the way of rules for determining when you use these, a few examples might help.

- **What are you up to?** You know your wife is planning a birthday surprise but you don't know what it is.

- **What are ye up to?** It's your children who are planning the surprise.

- **What are yiz up to?** It's your children again, but this time it's not your birthday and you are worried.

- **What are yous up to?** Same children, but less worried and more angry.

- **I love you:** For your parent, partner, spouse or child.

- **I love ye:** For either your parents or your children, particularly when they surprise you with a wonderful gift like a car, cake, holiday away or have simply not destroyed the house in your absence.

- **I love yiz:** For your mates (particularly female) after a feed of drink.

- **I love yous:** For your mates (particularly male) after a feed of drink.

SO I AM

Finally, Irish people love confirmation, both the religious ceremony where you swear to God you won't drink alcohol until you're 14, 18 or 45 (the age may vary) as well as the warm approval we get when we say something agreeable. In fact, when it comes to this verbal endorsement, we love confirmation so much we often do it ourselves.

As a result, it is not unusual to hear Irish people say something and then confirm it themselves immediately after.

— I am completed stuffed, **so I am**.

— I forgot all about it, **so I did**.

— I'll ask her to marry me, **so I will**.

— I love you, **so I do**.

SCHOOL

—

Though there are many places in Ireland that have uniquely Irish words or expressions, few have such concentrations as you might find in an Irish school starting with the actual types of school we have in Ireland.

TYPES OF SCHOOL

PRIMARY SCHOOL: This is the first proper stage of school from about four or five up to that moment when children stop being all cute and lovable. Primary schools today generally come in three main forms. The first are religious-run schools beginning with a saint's name, like Mary, Michael, Peter, Patrick or Paul, the second are Irish language schools called 'Gaelscoils' where the saint's name is as Gaeilge, and the third are secular or 'Educate Together' schools. Of course, in the religious-run schools children are indeed 'educated together', but the main difference is that here they spend an additional year learning to bless themselves and sing 'Here I Am Lord' in unison while their secular friends use this time to collect leaves to trace into their copies.

SECONDARY SCHOOL: While this may sound like a place for those who just weren't cut out for primary school, it is in fact what most other countries call high school. In Ireland, secondary schools are either private schools (the minority) or not-private schools (the majority). We don't call them public schools. While there is a range of secondary schools, a few names are worth knowing.

◆ **The Brothers:** Less a big happy family looking out for each other and more like Goodfellas with collars. The traditional all-boys schools of Ireland that were run by a group of mixed martial arts fighters, also known as the Christian Brothers. Most Brothers are no longer run by Brothers, whose numbers have dwindled since the setting up of the RICO Act. Or maybe I'm still thinking of Goodfellas?

◆ **The Convent:** All big towns have a school called the Convent. Very few convent schools have serving nuns still working in them, and those that do tend to be the ones who are really quite small, always smiling and watering the plants.

◆ **Mercy:** Not what you shout as you begin to lose consciousness, but the all-girls schools which were the traditional rivals of the Convent, unless of course, they were the Convent!

◆ **The Tech:** As in the technical college or VEC. This used to be the toughest school in town and the traditional rivals of the Brothers.

CLASSROOM & SCHOOLYARD SPEAK

Long before words like numeracy, literacy, critically reflective and learning practitioner came into use, schools used a selection of some very different words. Here is a selection.

◆ **Mitch:** Not the German chart-topping heartthrob of *Baywatch* fame, but what you occasionally did during double French. While Mitch from *Baywatch* could be found in the mid-'90s on the beaches of Malibu, mitchers from Irish schools in the mid-'90s could usually be found down the fields, behind the castle or in bed while their parents were at work.

◆ **On the hop:** The same as mitching, but this was when you were gone for the whole day and kept having to change locations like safe houses so you wouldn't be caught.

◆ **Wedgie:** Neither a hipster's chip nor exclusive to Ireland, the wedgie was an early form of male contraception in Catholic Ireland whereby the briefs, boxers or underpants were pulled upwards past the corduroy trousers until they either ripped or the woodwork teacher came in.

◆ **Cog:** Sounds like a vital tooth of a rotating gear without which it would inevitably break down. In Irish schools, it was the practice of avoiding detention by copying the homework of another student because you were watching the match last night and forgot to do it.

◆ **Mála/marla:** There is a school of thought that suggests it was the use of 'mála' in the classroom that enabled Ireland to get out from under the yoke of both British imperialism and the Irish Catholic Church. Whatever the truth of this, mála – the Irish version of plasticine that came in 100 different colours, all of them brown – was perhaps one of the most ground-breaking, influential and fun classroom activities we grew up with as kids, even if all we ever made were snakes, worms and draft excluders. Importantly, whether you call it mála or marla will usually indicate your socio-economic level; what side of the Shannon you were born on; and whether you are from a Fianna Fáil house of a Fine Gael one!

◆ **Locks:** Neither a mechanical device used to secure items of importance or a contraption for canals but the short tuft of hair parked in front of your ear. Just as Achilles had his heel and Samson had his hair, Christian Brother students had their locks. It was the ultimate weak spot which male teachers would often pull on for misdemeanours that ranged from not having homework done to the fact they just didn't like you.

◆ **Deadner:** Sometimes called a 'dead arm', this is the limp, throbbing sensation you get in your arm when a class-mate who you know will grow up to become a guard punches you just below the shoulder.

◆ **Dead-butt:** What many a young man dreamed of during lunchtime! Thankfully this referred to the skilful throw of a ball against a wall so that it would strike it at the exact spot where it met the ground, thus making it bounce back in a roll along the ground. If you ever played handball you'd understand.

◆ **Roofing:** Another handball-related term that might make a board of management worry. However, it is not a precursor for a publicly damaging court case involv-ing a student party but the annoying practice whereby a student (always either older or tougher) would throw your slightly awry handball over a nearby roof, forcing the owners to race around before it was robbed on them.

◆ **Backer:** One of the most common forms of (pre-social media/parents driving you 400 yards in their SUV) assisted school transport where you'd tag a lift off a mate by sitting either on their bike rack (sore) or along their crossbar (less sore but more intimate).

◆ **Sketch!:** You could be forgiven for thinking that this is the opening shout of a quick-fire life-drawing contest. However, you'd be wrong. It is in fact the warning call of the Irish teenager when a member of the teaching staff is spotted in the vicinity of mitching, cogging, smoking or wedgie-ing. If heard outside the school just swap the teachers for guards.

◆ **Staish!:** Same as 'sketch' except further north.

◆ **Lick-arse:** Those irritating feckin' students who put up their hands and answer questions in class. Basically the bright ones who will be successful in life.

◆ **Topper:** This was an old word we used for the pencil sharpener that we no longer use anymore because a) we call them pencil-parers and b) we don't really use pencils anymore. This is a pity, because there were few other reasons why students could just randomly get up out of their seats and go for a wander except when saying they needed to pare their pencil.

◆ **Rubber:** What we used to call an eraser. This has also gone the way of the topper, but this is due more to the fact that in the 21st century teachers get mildly uncomfortable asking the class if anyone has a rubber they can lend little Johnny.

IRiSH
WE WiLL
NEVER FORGET

A big part of the schooling system in Ireland is the learning of the native language, Gaeilge (Irish). Unfortunately, despite being taught it for 23 out of the 14 years we spend in the Irish education system, knowledge of our own language remains miserably low. That said, there are certain Irish words and phrases that the Irish education system will never let us forget and which can occasionally turn up in conversation without causing confusion. Our top 10.

10.

Anseo: Meaning 'here'. This was the universal student response on hearing their names being called out by teachers at the beginning of the day. So ingrained was our response to hearing our name called out that North Korean re-education schools would have found it difficult to preprogramme a different response. To this day, it is amazing to see just how many seven-year olds will chirp out 'anseo' if you sneak up behind them in a shopping centre and call their name in an authoritative tone. Not that we do.

9.

Ciúnas!: 'Silence!' This is what was shouted out at the beginning of class to get us to pay attention and again whenever we fell around laughing because someone farted.

8.

Is maith liom: 'I like'. This phrase was the mainstay of oral Irish examinations for many students. When asked a question, the student would desperately try to swing the conversation to something they liked before offering a list as long as your arm of other things they liked. 'Is maith liom ... agus is maith liom ... agus is maith liom....'

7.

Fuinneog: 'Window'. A favourite household accessory partly for the fact that it sounded so removed from the word it described.

6.

Cáca milis: 'Cake'. Number-one foodstuff that people 'maith'-ed, as in 'Is maith liom cáca milis'. While it is an urban myth that countless women in the likes of Rome, Reykjavik and Rio were pulled by an Irishman spouting 'Is maith liom cáca milis', such a phrase regularly crops up amongst the paragraph of Irish that people can remember when trying to show others what speaking Irish sounds like. 'Ronan Ó Mordha is ainm dom. Tá muinteor agam. Ta dhá dheathair agam agus aon dheirfuir. Tá mé ina chonaí í mBaile Átha Troim. Is maith liom cáca milis.'

5.

Chúaigh me síos an staighre: 'I went down the stairs'. One of our favourite expressions for how we began our day every morning, even if the majority of us lived in bunga-lows. This was the moment in class when our level of Irish dialogue took on a brief fluency that made us feel proud of our native tongue. It didn't last long as we tried to explain what we then ate for breakfast.

4.

Bainne: 'Milk'. Even the sound of it brings images of cold, fresh, white milk on a hot summer's day. 'Bainne', the drink of gods. Okay, maybe that's ambrosia, but milk is a good substitute. If the sound of milk brings refreshing mental images on a hot summer's day, then 'bainne' is an altogether even more positive picture. After 'cáca milis', 'báinne' is the most popular food item rudimentary Gaelic speakers like to like – 'agus is maith liom bainne'.

3.

Bualadh bos: 'A round of applause'. This is what the teacher gave us when we got all our spellings right, knew all the lakes of Ireland or kept the colours between the lines.

2.

Uisce beatha: Literally, 'water of life'. Actually, 'whiskey'. The best Irish word we ever learnt, even better than 'gnéas'.

1.

An bhfuil cead agam dul go dtí an leithreas: 'Can I have permission to go to the bathroom'. Being able to say this is why 52% of people put down on the census form that they are able to speak Irish. Being able to put **más é do thoil é**, 'if you please', is why 15% of those 52% add fluently.

EXAM TIME

Of course, school was not only a time of boredom, homework, detention, making friends, lunchtime kick-abouts and oh ... the love of learning. We also had exams to look forward to. Despite each sounding like a different type of sleeping arrangement, these were in fact real evidence that the student in question had failed their **mocks*** and were finally realising that they were screwed.

GETTING THE HEAD DOWN: This happens when the student finally realises they have absolutely no idea how to write a letter to their French pen pal or describe the achievements of any inter-party coalition. As a result, they have no choice but to confirm to their friends that they are not staying out to play kerbs because they're – deep breath – 'getting the head down'.

LYING LOW: Having decided to get the head down, said student would disappear except for rare sightings on early mornings when they went out for air or to get their mother a litre of milk. At this point they would be 'lying low'.

DOING AN ALL-NIGHTER: Finally, with only hours to go until the first English exam, the student would shoot up on coffee and cornflakes and 'do an all-nighter', when he/she would overdose on any remaining information.

* Mocks: The practice run at the Leaving Certificate exams.

FOOD
AND
DRINK

—

When it comes to food, though we might not be world-famous, Europe-famous or even Irish-famous, there are plenty of foodstuffs whose names can cause a little confusion to those unfamiliar with them.

BiSCUiTS

- **Biscuits:** No, not for the dog, but for the person. Americans call them cookies. We call them biscuits and they go with tea.

- **Fig rolls:** Neither made of figs nor looking like rolls, fig rolls were an Irish tradition until someone found out they weren't Catholic.

- **Snack:** If you ask in a pub if they serve snacks, don't be surprised if you are left holding a pink or yellow biscuit bar that according to some ceased production back in 1992 but still find their way into local bars across the country.

BREAD

Sliced pan: In the *Terminator* series of movies, cyborgs are identified by dogs barking at them. In Ireland, they are given away by how they say 'it's the best thing since sliced bread', because as everyone knows we say 'sliced pan' here in Ireland instead.

Batch loaf: A 'batch loaf' is like a sliced pan except a little taller, making it more difficult to fit in your back pocket, with a well-fired crust on top. Because it is cooked in batches, hence the name, and then torn apart, it has no side crusts.

Turnover: Originally called the 'stuck-together' until they were sued by a crap boy band, the 'turnover' is similar to the batch except only two sides need to be torn away once baked. Popular in Dublin for its ability to be squashed into a ball really easily.

Brown bread: Also known by the more politically correct term of soda bread, brown bread is what every family has a recipe for and which is often made with soda powder instead of yeast.

Blaa: Originating in Waterford, this soft white roll dusted with flour is a protected food species, like feta, champagne and wild pandas. A 'blaa' goes well with breakfast, soup or anyone from the Deise.

Potato cake: Sometimes known as 'potato farl', neither tasting very potato-like nor looking very cake-like, 'potato cakes' are just one more example of how Irish people can eat potatoes at any time of the day and in any way.

Barm brack: Also known as 'bair-brack', you tend to come across this yeasted bread with raisins and sultanas around Halloween. Only at this time of year can you stick rings, coins, hairs and sticky plasters in processed food without fear of complaints and claim that they are there intentionally.

Boxty: Yes, you guessed it, more potato. This time, this is your traditional potato pancake, which, due to its flour content, can also call itself bread.

Sangwich: No, you haven't misheard anything, it's just the way some Irish people pronounce 'sandwich'. Can also be pronounced 'sangitch'.

Sambo: Just like a 'sangwich' but doesn't take as long to prepare.

Breakfast roll: Several types of pig with an egg in a bread roll. Helped fuel the Celtic Tiger.

MEAT

- **Stew:** Meat and root vegetables cooked together preferably for days with a drop of Guinness in it for no harm.

- **Crubeens:** Pig's trotters. Taste lovely but not a first-date dinner.

- **Coddle:** Sounds romantic, but with every bit of the pig floating in it, is anything but.

- **Pudding:** Basically much of the leftovers of the pig, which is either black (due to the inclusion of blood) or white (due to the exclusion of blood). Thought to be what Michael Jackson was referring to.

NON-MEAT

- **Colcannon and champ:** This isn't the name of a male duo who scored three top ten singles in the mid-1960s, but rather mashed potatoes with either cabbage, butter and milk or scallions, butter and milk.

ALCOHOLIC DRINKS

Porter: Basically Guinness.

Stout: Basically Guinness.

Black stuff: Basically Guinness.

Guinness and blackcurrant: Popular drink for 70-year-old women and American tourists who want to persevere in drinking the black stuff but can't quite stomach the taste.

Smithwicks: An Irish red ale that is older than Guinness. For the love of God, don't pronounce the 'w' when you order it!

Irish coffee: Almost exactly like normal coffee with brown sugar, cream and ... oh yeah ... whiskey.

Hot whiskey: Best consumed on cold December nights, a hot whiskey is made up of whiskey, boiling water, cloves, lemon, sugar/honey and happiness. While barmen are almost always accommodating in preparing you one, ordering a round of these half an hour before midnight on New Year's Eve might get you thrown out.

Poitín: Illegally home-made alcohol usually derived from barley that is exceptionally strong. Traditionally used for shocking news, cows undergoing a difficult calving and flesh wounds.

Fat Frogs: Never get into buying rounds with someone who is buying Fat Frogs. Air travel to continental Europe can cost less! Thankfully Fat Frogs, which are a mix of Smirnoff Ice, Bacardi Breezer and Blue WKD, are almost extinct since the country went bankrupt and half a generation took off for Australia.

TWO SPECIALITIES WE DON'T DRINK

BLACK AND TAN: A mixture of Guinness and lager named after the not-so-fun fellows of the Royal Irish Constabulary Force sent to Ireland in the 1920s to tear strips off us.

IRISH CAR BOMB: Don't let the Irish ingredients – Bailey's cream, Irish whiskey and Guinness – fool you. We don't drink this in Ireland so don't ask. This is partly due to fact that whiskey and Bailey's cream quickly curdle when mixed and partly because of its name. I mean really, do you think we'd make a 'Twin Towers' cocktail and expect Americans to drink it?!

SOFT DRINKS

★ **Mineral:** Mineral is the catch-all term that Irish people use to refer to non-alcoholic soft drinks such as lemonade, cola and fizzy orange. Just like yer wan's sex tape, all references to how minerals got their name have been deleted from the internet. It was once perfectly acceptable in the 1980s to throw the keys of your Fiat Mirafiori on the bar counter and order a pint of stout and a baby Hennessey along with some 'minerals' for the kids. Of course, this is thankfully no longer acceptable due to the stigma attached with owning a Mirafiori.

★ **MiWadi:** Miwadi is Ireland's premier soft drink concentrate. With a name coming from the company that it is derived from, **Mi**neral **Wa**ter **Di**stributors, 'MiWadi' is one of the annual St Paddy's presents given to the US President behind closed doors – though no one will admit it. More than this, it is an exceptionally popular drink to order when watching the Merseyside Derby or provincial final on a Sunday afternoon. Proper pubs don't charge you for this.

★ **Rock Shandy:** The official soft drink of the middle classes, a 'Rock Shandy' is half Club Lemon, half Club Orange. Though they are as expensive as a double brandy, buying a round of these for the nieces and nephews will make you 'relative gold'.

★ **Red lemonade:** Someone has probably been over this with you already. It is red, it's not really lemonade and I hear the present Pope is fond of it. What's not to like?

★ **Cidona:** A tasty type of apple juice that was once considered the gateway drink to cider.

NiGHT-TiME FOOD

Spice burger: Neither a burger in the conventional sense nor spicy in the conventional sense. The last person who actually knew what these things were died in 1982.

Snack box: Old night-time favourite. A 'snack box' is a paper box filled with fried chicken and chips. Interestingly, it is the only food that has ever been sued. A man from Thurles brought a civil action case that went all the way to the Supreme Court, arguing that the snack box was not actually a snack but a meal. Despite showing more than a dozen unfinished snack boxes he had collected over a four-month period, he lost and had to pay costs.

Battered sausage: A sausage (using the term liberally) coated, drizzled, smothered and welded into a bed of batter.

Boardsmill: A battered sausage with a trail of onions along it.

Battered burger: As if there weren't enough mouth-watering ways to prepare for a heart attack, a 'battered burger' is exactly that: a burger in batter.

Whirly burger: What you eat to kid yourself into thinking that it's not that unhealthy to have a battered burger as long as it's in a bun with all the dressings.

Three-in-one: Fast-tracked in the 1980s by An Bord Pleanála to help boost a declining Irish food industry, the 'three-in-one' has been a favourite for nigh on two generations. Part carb, part curry, part carb, the three-in-one is the essential mix of rice, chips and curry sauce. What's not to like?

Rissoles: In France these are small croquettes. In Wexford they do away with that posh-sounding nonsense and recreate them in the form of battered (or breaded) mashed chips. Until recently it was an offense to bring them out of the county.

Taco fries: Sounds like Mexico, looks like Tijuana, more dangerous than Juarez. Chips with some sort of meat that is hard to make out with the amount of sauce and cheese on top. In a recent survey it was discovered that only 3% of those who order taco fries are actually sober.

One 'n' one: Meaning one fish and one chips.

Spice bag: Introduced originally to counter the zebra mussel problem in the Shannon basin, 'spice bags' had gained a foothold in the post-drink food culture by at least 2013. Since then, this food made up of fried chicken something, fried chicken something else, fried bits of vegetables, fried chicken something, chips and some mysterious spice mined in Carlow has begun to take over the slot once occupied by the three-in-one. Kind of like the grey squirrel versus red squirrel thing.

EATING

Possibly due to our chequered history of eating food or not eating it (see: The Famine), many of our words relating to food involve us eating it at a pace similar to wild bald eagle chicks that don't want to be the malnourished one who's not going to make it.

ALP: When you turn away for a moment only to turn back around to see your son has just 'alped down his dinner'.

GOBBLE: This is sometimes a term of pride employed by parents when describing how their little one has 'gobbled' up their dinner in under two minutes.

WOLF: You're late for training, for the train or for Tríona, and you make the decision that it's better to have something in your stomach than not. As a result, whatever food is in front of you, you just 'wolf' it down.

HORSE (IT INTO YOU): Used by hosts for guests who at first didn't have time to stay for food, but considering it is already made and would go to waste otherwise, have now sat down. Just 'horse it into you', they might say as their visitor desperately tries to eat a Sunday lunch two hours before their plane takes off.

DRINKING

SUP: While a 'sup' also represents a little drinkeen like a small glass of whiskey, 'to sup' is to drink something slowly and steadily, trying not to sound unmannerly.

GULP: This is what children across the country are warned not to do, especially when it comes to soft drinks.

SKULL: Usually associated with alcohol, 'to skull' something is to consume it one go. Skulling a pint is one of the best wastes of €5 today as well as being puerile, silly and frankly irresponsible. Therefore, if you are a global star visiting Ireland, you will become an instant hero!

NECK: Like skulling except when you drink a bottle of beer in one go. Impressive up until the age of 19.

DOWN: When someone buys you a disgusting shot you have to drink in one go because it's your birthday, their birthday or someone else's birthday.

KNOCK IT BACK: While 'knock it back' can be used for an alcoholic drink, it is also employed for that nasty-tasting medicine prescribed to clear your cough.

SPORT (FOOTBALL)

—

The Irish love sport and of all the sports in Ireland, two of the most popular are 'football' and 'football'. Of course, when we say the first 'football' we are talking about Gaelic football, or 'gaaaaa' (GAA) to the non-Gaelic-football-playing public. And when we say the second 'football', we are of course talking about soccer. Despite years of research centreing on intonation, facial cues, pheromones and body language, it is impossible to identify which 'football' the person is referring to when they say they have 'football' training this evening. That said, there is a number of terms, quite unique to Ireland, that might help give it away.

FOOTBALL (MEANING GAELIC) TERMS

- **Forty-five:** Gaelic football's corner-kick, except not taken in the corner.

- **Junior C:** Where young and old footballers pass each other in this great sport.

- **Back against forwards:** Staple of GAA football training for nigh on three generations.

- **Maor uisce:** This means water boy, but is actually the person who will most likely be suspended for six months for getting involved in the pitch-side brawl.

- **Field:** Not only where the game is played, but the art of leaping high, high into the air to catch the ball from a kick-out.

- **Back door:** The exceptionally unofficial term used to describe how teams can re-join the championship after they lose.

- **Solo:** How you travel up the field with the ball by either dropping the ball onto your toe and back into your hands as you run, which you can intersperse with a bounce.

- **Han Solo:** The coolest character in Star Wars, along with Chewbacca. Decent full-back too.

- **Umpire:** Not the referee, but four of his assistants who wear white jackets and wave flags at him. Don't ask.

- **Square ball:** An oxymoron used to describe the most infuriating foul a full-forward can give away.

- **Take your points and the goals will come:** A common phrase on the GAA pitch, meaning to take the easy scores and the big scores will come. Since then its usage has spread and it isn't unusual to overhear it in Coppers.

- **Small ball:** Not Gaelic football at all, but rather its sibling, hurling – that most magnificent spectacle of sporting art that involves hurleys, sliothars and sweat.

OTHER 'SMALL BALL' TERMS

- **Sliotar:** What the leather ball used in hurling is called.

- **Puck:** How the sliotar is passed from one hurley stick to the next.

- **Bas:** The flattened, curved end of the hurley that you'll feel if it strikes you across the thigh.

- **Dual player:** Not someone who takes part in a misspelt arranged combat engagement, but someone who plays both hurling and football.

- **Plenty of hurls on the line:** A polite way of saying don't be afraid to break a few.

FOOTBALL (MEANING SOCCER) TERMS

- **Hoof:** The bastion of the team that is getting beaten badly. When you just can't hold possession and the ball breaks to you, just hoof up it away.

- **Hatching:** This was a mortal sin in a game of football when a player, usually a Sheffield Wednesday fan for some reason, would hang around your goal in the hope that the ball would be 'hoofed' up to them for a sneaky put-away goal.

- **Fluke:** When you attempt to pull off a cross-field pass but slice it off the side of your HiTecs and score instead.

- **Balloon:** When you strike for the goal but put the ball some 15 metres over the imaginary crossbar. Chances of this increase dramatically when you are five metres out

from the goal with no one around you, but everyone (including the girl you fancy but never had the guts to ask out) looking on.

- **Roasted:** How you describe what has happened to you when the guy you have been tasked with marking has scored two and set up another all within the first 15 minutes.

- **Big-toe:** Smashing the ball with the point of your foot. Very effective for penalty kicks though despised by the opposition.

- **House:** As in 'mind your house'. Shouted to warn your teammate of an incoming opposition player who was as likely to deftly dispossess you as he was to go through you with both boots.

- **Stinger:** Getting the ball smashed against your thigh. Occurrences of this increased four fold during the first five minutes of games played on cold days.

- **First pick!:** Probably the most important two words in a school football game when someone initiated the game by declaring they had first pick. Inevitably the proven goal-scoring midfield who was a year older than everyone would be chosen.

- **Next goal wins:** Common shout to bring a game close to an end when the game is either locked at 14–14 and *Home and Away* is starting, or it is not locked at 14–2 but the losing team have had enough and you want to keep them out for one more goal.

- **World Cup:** This is the quintessential kick-about game. It has absolutely nothing to do with the FIFA World Cup except for the ball. Rules are: One player who is either injured or crap gets put in goals, then every outfield player must score a goal to qualify for the next round until one player is left, who then gets knocked out. Epic games of this went on for weeks.

- **No lashing it (no belting):** This was the sacrifice or rider that was needed to ensure any kick-about had a goal-keeper. Because hardly anyone ever wanted to be a goalkeeper, you had to promise if they went in there would be 'no lashing it'.

OTHER GAMES

There are of course many other non-football games that can be played in Ireland, but a few children's games that are more particular to the country include the following.

KERBS: In some quarters of the world, hearing that your child is out all evening playing 'kerbs', might send hearts a-racing. However, in Irish estates, 'kerbs' was a memorable mainstay of summer fun as two players on adjacent pavements threw a football across at each other in the hope of hitting the edge of the 'kerb'.

IRISH BULLDOG: Like British Bulldog, except, er ... substitute the word 'Irish' for 'British'. A cousin of another English game, Red Rover, sometimes called 'Madra Rua' in hard-core republican schoolyards, Irish Bulldog involved one person stuck in the middle of the yard/park/field as participants ran past. Anyone he or she caught joined them and this continued until someone dislocated a shoulder trying to rugby through 18 of their peers.

TIP THE CAN: A more sophisticated version of chase where the person chasing must spot their targets and make it back to the 'can' before their opponent. The 'can' may be anything from an ESB box to an elder tree (but never, ever a can).

GiVING SOMETHING A TRY

Ireland and success have never been ready bedfellows, whether it be in history, in sport or in sustaining long periods of steady economic growth. When it comes to giving things a go, however, whether in sport or elsewhere, the Irish are a great people at giving something a try. Unsurprisingly, then, we have several terms that we use in such situations.

Give it a lash: Aside from being a great name for a beauticians, 'giving it a lash' is perhaps the nation's favourite. The phrase came to national attention when, back in 1990, the Irish football team and canny fly-fisherman Jack Charlton were urged on by the Irish people to give the World Cup a lash. And, in fairness, they did get all the way to the quarter-finals.

Give something a go: Used for when, on your partner's advice, you try crochet or nicotine patches or waxing.

Have a blast at it: One that is often heard at sing-songs and lock-ins when someone takes up an old fiddle, a bodhrán or a music-box and 'has a blast' at someone's request.

Give something your best shot: What parents say to their children, especially when the parents know that their child is the slowest thing to hit the racetrack since a wet Wednesday afternoon last November.

Sure, fire away so: Said by someone who has spent a fruitless half hour trying to get the car to start, settle the little one or finish the crossword. In such circumstances, they will turn to their supportive partner and tell them, 'sure, fire away so', confident in the knowledge that they'll have no luck either. When they do start the car, settle the wee one and come up with that seven-letter word for puzzled beginning with 'B', their partner will thank them and then resent them for the rest of the evening.

Let rip: Where you just decide to take the handbrake off (metaphorically) and give it everything you've got. It is often done on the encouragement of an uncle, 'G'wan John, let rip at it'.

Take a crack at it: Often used by confident young men taking part in a quiz or competition irrespective of how unlikely they are to name the capital of Australia (no, it's not Sydney, Seán) or correctly guess the weight of the prize bull in their local agricultural show.

ONWARDS TO VICTORY

Of course, there is no point giving something a go unless you have a wide range of colourful expressions that those shouting you on to success can use.

Maigh Eo abú!: Or whatever county you support. 'Abú' means forever, or 'to victory'. However, possibly because the country has not had a rich history of victories, its use is not as common as you might expect. That said, in the last few years it has made a big comeback, particularly in and around western Gaelic grounds.

Up you boyo!: The perfect shout as the corner-forward loops another well-earned point over the bar to extend the lead and make you believe you are finally going to win.

C'mon to f*!:** When, a quarter of an hour later, you're now four points down with five minutes to go. Add or subtract exclamation marks depending on the number of points and minutes remaining.

Go on you good thing!: Common expression heard around the racetrack as your horse clears the last fence, pulls alongside the frontrunner and is let off the bridle. Not so appropriate when it is humans running around the race-track. Can also be employed as **g'wan ya good thing!**

DESCRiBiNG STUFF

—

Whether you are living here or just visiting, it is important to be able to describe whatever you get up to. The following section should help.

DESCRIBING QUANTITIES

When describing quantities, aside from the number of people in a pub, there are several terms Irish people use alongside full, empty and half full.

Hape: This signifies a great amount of and is a particularly good description for something that is in a pile, like a 'hape of sand', 'a hape of potatoes' or a 'hape of silage'.

Wojus: Had it been an Irishman who wrote the Bible it would not have been a 'plague of locusts' but a 'wojus amount of locusts'. Wojus, also known as woegus, is a voluminous sum that no amount of arm-stretching can possibly describe.

Full to the knickers: Exceptionally full. For instance, you might have your car tank 'full to the knickers', meaning that even if you shake it a little you won't get another five cents in. Or you might have the car so 'full to the knickers' while moving house you can't fit another toilet brush in for fear of having the suspension drag along the ground.

Rake: Most commonly used to describe the amount of pints consumed last night, 'a rake of something' is used in much the same way as a 'hape'.

The whole shebang: This is when you include everything. If you sold your car and told the person that for €5,000 they could have 'the whole shebang', you'd mean everything from the wobble-head dog and the pine freshener to the Norah Jones CD and the spare change down the seat.

The works: Often used with food. For example a burger with 'the works', means absolutely everything on it, including the pickle.

Dollop: A 'dollop' is a large spoonful of something that probably isn't good for you but tastes great.

DESCRiBiNG DiSTANCES

When it comes to distances, as well as using your regular array of metric and imperial units, several other ways of assessing distances can be heard.

- **Within an ass's roar:** This is a very far distance away. In metaphorical terms, it is a guess that wasn't even close, like naming Shergar as the first animal to go into space. In GAA terms, an ass's roar is about 40 yards wide of the posts.

- **Spitting distance and a stone's throw:** Probably a little more than actual spitting distance or a stone's throw – but not by much.

- **Mighty:** A serious distance that will take you all day to get to.

- **Mile:** While a mile, as all know, is akin to 1,609 metres, if someone indicates to you that what you are looking for is 'just a mile up the road' one thing you can probably be sure of is that it is a lot further that 1,609 metres up the road. If they give it in kilometres then you're probably all right.

DESCRIBING SOMETHING THAT IS GREAT

While we might have a lot of words for average, we have just as many for great.

- **Savage:** When someone says something, some time or somewhere was 'savage', you know they really mean it.

- **The business:** Describing something as 'the business' is like giving it 100% on Tripadvisor. You can also use the expression 'the biz'.

- **Serious:** 'Serious' means that it was a truly memorable event and you feel sorry that the person you are telling wasn't present for what was 'a serious party' or 'a serious game of hurling'.

- **The bee's knees:** While the 'bee's knees' enjoyed brief popularity during the Roaring Twenties in the US, in

Ireland we still like to employ the term for things, particularly to fads like playing Snake on your Nokia or Oxygen bars.

- **Cat's pyjamas:** Used in conjunction with the 'bee's knees' when you really want to emphasise that the fad is really worth doing.

- **Mighty:** Often used by someone who has a great big grin across their face staring upwards to the heavens; 'it was mighty altogether', as if the Lord himself had been involved.

- **Bang on:** If something is 'bang on' then it has hit the spot or is spot on, whether it be a cold pint on a hot summer's day or a perfectly level shelf you've just hung. 'That's bang on, so it is'.

- **Deadly:** Thankfully this does not actually mean 'deadly' as in box-jellyfish deadly, but it does in fact mean 'deadly' as in great fun. It is interesting to note that there are two types of deadly – there is 'deadly' and then there is 'bleedin' deadly', with both particularly popular in and around the capital.

- **Buzz:** Usually seen in the company of 'deadly', as in 'deadly buzz', meaning brilliant fun altogether.

- **Class:** Meaning much the same as 'deadly', 'class' basically means brilliant. Perhaps our favourite ever use of the word was by our own Jimmy Magee when he described Diego Armando Maradona's second goal against England back in 1986 as a 'different class, different classsssss!'

- **Massive:** To be 'massive' is the dream of many a young lady, especially in Dublin. Having absolutely nothing to do with the amount of physical space you take up, 'massive' actually refers to the state of being brilliant, beautiful, lovely, smashing, class! What your wan Aoife Dooley is.

- **Game-ball:** Means perfect, couldn't be better, as in 'How's the job going? Ah, game-ball'.

- **Unreal:** Often pronounced 'Unnn-realllll', this encapsulates a really great occurrence that, while hoped for, was never really thought possible. I mean, Paul McGrath turning up at your house to wish you a happy 11th birthday, absolutely unnn-realllll so it was!

- **The best night ever!:** Obviously describing a period of time, this is not just a decent evening of fun but 'the best night ever'. This is a favourite with those trying to make you feel jealous because you pulled out at the last minute.

- **Gas:** Something that 'is gas' is great craic and laugh-out-loud funny.

- **That's moon:** Like gas except moon.

🌙 **Epic:** Epic is what we say for something that is truly ... well ... 'epic'. It basically describes something that is truly 11/10. For instance, an epic night out would be one where you plan on a couple of drinks and to be in bed by midnight but end up crossing the border, partying until dawn and ending up with four types of currency in your back pocket. By the time you wake up the clocks have gone forward, you're on first names terms with Paraguayan emigration and have made three friends for life. 'Epic!'

DESCRIBING THE BAD STUFF

While pointing out that something is 'shite' is a very common way to identify something as being bad or well below par, we have a multitude of other ways to say something is less than what was hoped for.

Cac: Despite this being Irish for shit, something that is 'cac' is usually not as bad as its organic counterpart and isn't a complete write-off. For example, you will usually finish watching a movie even if is 'cac'. If, however, something is 'pure cac', like a bad-tasting pint, then you should definitely get rid of it.

Gick: Like 'cac' except usually worse or smellier.

Gammy: Usually distinguishes something that is not working properly. You could have a 'gammy' foot, a 'gammy' washing machine or a 'gammy' wheelbarrow, all of which are useless and should be gotten rid of (except maybe the foot; you might just get this looked at).

Cat: While in some isolated pockets of the country, something that is described as 'cat' means incredible, for most of us, something that's 'cat' is terrible. It could be describing the weather, the food, the pint, the performance, the person, or indeed pretty much anything.

Wile: More of a negative adjective to emphasise something bad. For example, you might say 'wile bad' or 'wile windy'.

Lousy: A common term, particularly for something that is just pure bad, like when your older sister flushes away half of your new football stickers because you ate all the Celebrations.

Malogin: While 'malogin' has more noms de plume than an international art thief – 'malojan', 'malowgin', 'malogen', 'melodeon', 'mologen' – each one generally means the same thing: crap. Growing up, two things often tended to be 'malogin altogether', the weather and the TV reception for BBC 2.

Cat malogin: This was the perfect storm when, not only were you stuck indoors because it was lashing outside, but the TV reception for every channel was gone. In these instances, it was 'cat malogin', i.e. terribly bad.

Poyzone: Little known east-coast amalgamation of poison and boy band Boyzone that signified something was terrible in that cheesy, I-can't-believe-you-said-that type of way, as in, 'that's Poyzone so it is!'

Desperate: Something awful which should make the person responsible for it feel wholly embarrassed and ashamed, for example 'That was a desperate performance', 'This music is desperate', or 'Them pants is desperate on ya.'

Hack: Dublin-centric statement that usually describes something that looks terrible altogether. For instance, you could complain about the 'hack' of your face if the make-up has been a bit of a disaster or the 'hack' of your dress after someone spills a Tia Maria down it.

Brutal: Much like desperate, this multi-functional term is used to describe the weather, the food, the accommodation or anything else that has made you regret the week's holiday in Salou.

Finally, to emphasise more fully that something is really bad, you can add any of the following words in front of it.

ONLY: Pretty bad.

TOTAL: Really bad.

PURE: Awfully bad.

COMPLETE: Terribly bad.

UTTER: 100% bad.

And then add the following word after.

... ALTOGETHER: Meaning there is no coming back from how bad it was.

DESCRIBING BAD STUFF

To state that something is disgusting we sometimes like to employ words that give a more prosaic view of the thing we are describing.

- **Mouldy:** While mouldy is of course best suited to some sort of foodstuff that has long since grown legs and gone off, mouldy can be used for anything that looks, smells or sounds nausea-inspiring.

- **Manky:** More commonly associated with something that smells terrible, from feet to food that just isn't cooked right.

DESCRIBING MISTAKES

Steve Staunton as Irish manager; the Millennium Clock; electronic voting; letting the Catholic Church run the country for its first 70 years; leaving it to Mrs O'Brien. Like any nation, Ireland is not exempt from making mistakes and we have made several. These mistakes can be categorised into some very Irishisms.

Hash: When you make a complete mess of something that is usually not that important. He made 'a right hash' of that parking, of that penalty, of that paella.

Hames: Where things start out okay only to completely unravel. Where 'hash' usually refers to the end product, 'hames' is commonly the present version of the 'hash' and as such might be recoverable if an expert takes over in time. For example, it could be a parent cutting her child's hair for the first time, someone cooking his first Christmas dinner or a lad trying to chat up a girl.

Complete bollix of it: Kind of like 'hash' but usually something much more important. Generally there is no way back when you make a 'complete bollix of something'.

Balls of it: How difficult can it be to cut your own hair? And then you found out. And as a result of getting the blades mixed up you've cut a runway across your scalp, 'making a balls of it'.

Cock-ups: 'Cock-ups' are employed for mistakes that are generally caused by one or more people getting their information wrong. It can be used for minor events, such as turning up for someone's retirement party a day early, to major events like the invading French army landing at the wrong end of the island in Kinsale.

Rag order: To leave something in 'rag order' is to leave something in such utter disarray that the person tasked with cleaning it up will be cursing you from now until Sunday.

Bags: When your attempt at fixing something becomes an utter disaster, like when you use white spirits to get some specks of paint off your nice sweater, only to de-colour the whole thing. In other words, 'you make a complete bags of it!'

GUBU: Grotesque, Unbelievable, Bizarre, Unprecedented. The term 'GUBU', coined in the early '80s, is a term used almost exclusively for political scandals.

Pig's ear: To make a 'pig's ear' of something is the type of mistake that children make, especially when doing their maths exam.

There are other words that can be used for mistakes and which we generally employ when identifying something as being wrong or out of place.

Skew-ways: When you're almost right but not quite, because you mixed left with right, top with bottom, or put the forks where the spoons go and the spoons where the knives go.

Arse-ways: Completely wrong. In fact, the person is so wrong that the end result will even confuse you as to what they were trying to achieve in the first place.

Backwards: Similar to skew-ways in that you end up seeing or doing something from the wrong direction. You go into a meeting expecting a raise but instead get sacked. You think you are being selected for full-forward but they wanted you to umpire instead. Or when you think you're in but then she tells you it's so good to count on you as a friend!

DESCRIBiNG EMBARRASSMENT

Hand-in-hand with making mistakes is the embarrassment that comes with them. Irish people hate to cause a scene, or at least they used to until they realised that they could put it up on the YouTube and people would give it a like! That said, people still get embarrassed, with the following words often used to describe it.

SCARLET: Sometimes used by the friend of the person who is embarrassed, as in 'scarlet for ya', this Dublin-based saying is perfect for when you are caught rapid doing something embarrassing.

MORTO: Short for mortified, 'morto' or 'pure morto' is most found in both Cork and Dublin and usually describes the utterer's reaction to situations that are dead embarrassing, like when their mother unexpectedly came home early.

HOLY SHOW: Strangely enough, it is usually not the child who is the 'holy show' after having a shouting match with their sibling in the supermarket, but the parent, hence the phrase, 'you've made a holy show of me'. You'll be in trouble when you get home and there'll be no raspberry ripple for a month.

A precursor to embarrassment is when you don't remember what it is that you did to be embarrassed about. Hearing the following phrases will usually give you a heads up.

THAT'S WHAT THEY'RE ALL SAYING: Who? What? Why? I didn't do anything! Very worrying.

EVERYONE IS TALKING ABOUT YOU: And you know why too! Not good.

YOU'RE THE TALK OF THE TOWN: Makes you feel uncomfortable but generally for good reasons like an engagement, a pregnancy or a bingo win.

A final set of phrases are those often used by parents for when they've actually caught or spotted you making a fool of yourself, at least in their eyes. You'll know this by the following.

WiLL YOU LOOK AT ...

... THE SET OF YA: More commonly used for under-12s who've been out in the yard, sandpit, garden or hay bales and have come home in an absolute mess.

... THE CUT OF YA: This for the over-12s and is particularly common when talking about the dress sense of a son or daughter on the way out to the pub. Interestingly, 'will you look at the cut of ya' can be used positively as well as negatively.

... THE STATE OF YA: You've drink taken and you thought by hooking your trousers onto the door handle of your parents' bedroom door they wouldn't notice your lack of sobriety and steadiness as you popped in to tell them you're fine. Instead you've stumbled, slipped and ended up almost wedgie-ing yourself a few inches off their floor. 'Will you look at the state of ya' your mother says and your father just grunts. You've let them down once again. Untie yourself and hang your head in shame, my friend, we've all been there.

DESCRIBING TIME

Along with seconds, minutes, weeks, days, months and years in Ireland we do have a number of additional time periods that we use on a regular basis.

~ **Jig time:** 'Jig time' is one of the fastest periods of times you can describe. Strangely enough, when someone says they will have something fixed, finished, collected or cooked in 'jig time' most people don't believe them, even though they nearly always prove them wrong.

~ **Forever:** It might seem strange that forever goes between jig time and a jiffy, but you need to understand that the people who use 'forever' are in a hurry and are reacting to the news that their spouse has to go in to grab milk in the supermarket and they're already late for mass/training/mass training. 'No way, sure that'll take forever!' It doesn't, it takes three-and-a-half minutes with the use of the self-service check-out.

~ **Jiffy:** To have something done in a 'jiffy' might sound a little crude, and in 4% of cases it probably is, but by and large it means to complete something, usually a favour, in a relatively short period of time. Items usually done in a 'jiffy' are often favours that you offer to do rather than force the person go to a professional like a mechanic, a plumber or a dentist. Consequently, it is worth noting that while quicker, allowing someone unqualified to fix your motor, install your new washing machine or pull out your loose tooth – 'sure why pay for it? I'll have it out in a jiffy' – might cost you in the long run.

~ **No time:** This is meant to symbolise the length of time it will take you to fix the puncture, have the lunch ready, go in and pick up the final essential ingredient for dinner, finish painting the gable wall etc. Anyone with a grain of sense will immediately begin to plan a fall-back, knowing that 'no time' is anywhere between 20 minutes and three-and-a-half days. There are actual stories of brides hearing the word 'no time' on the morning of their wedding day and being reduced to tears.

~ **Donkey's years:** 'Donkey's years' is used for when you meet an old friend and neither of you can remember exactly when it was you last met. In these cases you agree that it must have been 'donkey's years' ago.

~ **Aaages:** This is used regularly by children when complaining about having to sit in the car with their annoying sibling while Mam pops into the laundrette for a message and then ends up meeting Moira who fills her in on her daughter's engagement. You'll hear it in complaints like, 'Oh my God, you were aaages!' or pleas, as Mam goes into the butchers, 'don't be aaages, like the last time.'

~ **Yonks:** As in, 'I haven't heard from him in yonks'. 'Yonks' is a period of time so long that not only does no one actually know how long it represents – a year, a decade, a generation – no one can even remember when they last heard it being used. But they have heard it being used!

The movement of time is also an important part of daily conversation in Ireland, particularly how quickly the day actually is going. Indeed, in the annual straw poll of most popular break time conversations to have on a building site, 'how fast the day is going' usually finishes between 'the weather' and 'what the tea is like'.

~ **Flying by:** This is the quickest observation you can have during the day.

~ **Didn't see the morning go:** What to expect during the sales or when you actually enjoy your work!

~ **Hard to believe it's lunchtime already:** You can substitute Friday for lunchtime for the weekly observation.

~ **Dragging:** Often due to it raining outside all morning or because of the menial task you've been given.

~ **Slower than a wet week:** While it might sound almost impossible that an hour of work might feel slower than a wet week, that's what working on a conveyor belt can do for you.

DESCRIBING GOOD FORTUNE

A common phrase you might hear outside of Ireland is the 'luck of the Irish'. Strangely enough, despite 800 years of colonisation, the constant threat of rain, seasonal adjustment disorder, a famine and resulting emigration that led to the halving of the population, Irish people don't always see themselves as being that especially lucky. Still, we do have a few home-grown terms for good fortune all the same.

Flukey: This is where there seems to be little chance of success no matter how well the person performs, yet through the strangest quirks of fate they actually succeed. 'Talk about flukey' you are likely to hear in such situations. 'Flukes', like hole-in-ones, doubling the black or having yer wan say yes are generally considered once-offs, so make the most of them.

Jammy: Same as above, except the person shows no signs of skill or intelligence. It just happened. Scoring a goal when you are trying to cross, returning to your car on a busy city street to see you left the keys in the ignition or winning the lottery are all in the 'jammy' category.

A horseshoe stuck up your arse: Calls a jockey a jumper and thinks a horse that's well-handicapped has a low IQ, yet still manages to pick the winner of the Grand National.

Blessed: This term is generally employed to refer to the person who has that horseshoe stuck up their arse. Someone who is 'blessed' only studies one poet in the Leaving Cert yet still aces it; is at home hungover on the day their boss is off sick; or sleeps through their alarm the morning they were meant to set sail out of Cobh on the *Titanic*.

DESCRIBING MISFORTUNE

Now we're talking! Famine, failed revolt, months of scattered showers and sunny spells, Ireland is much more at home with a bit of misfortune than it is with some good luck. We have a couple of words to describe the calamity that has just befallen you.

Sickner: This small-scale misfortune occurs when a deadline is stopping you going out for a quick pint with friends, the boss has 'asked' you to work the Bank Holiday weekend or you get a puncture and the spare is also flat.

Bad sess: Meaning bad luck, 'bad sess' is particularly useful for food when you break the eggs on the way home from shopping, leave the milk out on that hot summer's day or drop the buttered hang sangwich and it opens and lands face down.

DESCRIBING A MESS

When something is in an utter state of untidiness then we usually call it a mess. In Ireland, there seems to be no end of things that can be in a mess – the boot of your car, your bedroom, your handbag or your love life. Unsurprisingly, with so many things that can fall into disarray, we do have several Irishisms that we can substitute for a 'mess'.

- **Tip:** This always refers to a specific place, most commonly your bedroom or your car and is frequently the result of an accumulation of dirty washing, empty food containers, product samples, training gear and a mysterious odour that you can't quite put your finger on.

- **Kip:** When you can put your finger on where the smell is coming from.

- **Rag order:** While this can sometimes refer to a place, it is more often used for something that is a mess because it has been left abandoned, uncleaned, unwashed or outside after its last use – a lawnmower, a paint brush, football boots. It is worth noting that there is always someone to blame for something being in 'rag order', although it is usually yourself.

... **Mank:** Similar to 'rag order', except 'mank' is a food-related mess. The dirty kebab you bought last night and dropped on the carpet when you came home – 'mank'. Forgetting to clean out the blender after that smoothie you made at the beginning of the week – 'mank'. Going away for a fortnight without cleaning out the opened yogurt from the fridge – 'mank'.

... **State:** Not to mixed up with the state of yer wan, 'a state' is a total mess that will take at least an hour to clean up. In terms of culprits, children under five are usually responsible for a place being in 'some state'; teenagers for leaving their room in a 'complete state'; the untrained puppy for turning the sitting room into 'an utter state'; and a stag party from the east leaving the B&B in 'an awful state'.

DESCRIBING THINGS

You know ... the thing ... that ... oh ... what's its name? Well, we have plenty of names for it in Ireland.

THINGY: This is what you call something you can see but you don't know the name of.

YOKE: This is what you call something you can't see and don't know the name of.

WHATCHAMACALLIT: When someone asks you about something you know well, you might even have done a degree on it, yet its name just escapes you. Interestingly, the use of 'whatchamacallit' has dropped dramatically with the explosion of smartphones and the Google.

THINGYMABOB OR THINGYMAJIG: In some way, people can still be divided between Roy Keane or Mick McCarthy; Collins or Dev; S Club 7 or Steps; Holy Communion in the palm of the hand or on the tongue. You either use thingymabob or thingymajig.

THE THINGYMAJIG: It is important not to mix 'thingymajig' with '*the* thingymajig'. The less said the better.

WORK

—

The Irish are known as an industrious bunch of people, both at home and also overseas. Every couple of generations, whole communities head over to England, Australia and America to dig ditches, work in mines or serve in armies. Unsurprisingly, we have the terminology to go with it.

WORK ETHIC

Irish people are unafraid of hard work and many a young Irish person has entered the workforce. Indeed, children as young as 12 can sometimes be spotted driving tractors along narrow country roads earning more money than trained professionals. This work ethic has spawned its own series of work-related Irishisms.

Tipping along: If there was one word for the type of work Irish people do, it would be 'tipping along'. While it might sound a little lazy, anyone who is 'tipping along' is steadily, systematically and comprehensively completing their work at just the right pace to be done by their deadline, no sooner or later.

Flying: When you come back from town to find your husband has the garden almost mowed, i.e. 'Jaysus, you're flying! You nearly have it all done, so you do!'

Hell for leather: Someone 'going hell for leather' is a person who is seriously going at it and has the type of work ethic you like to see in your staff. Give that person a raise!

Giving it socks: Similar to the person going hell for leather but perhaps not as well executed. 'In fairness to him, he was giving it socks, it's just a pity he knocked down half the wall while he was doing it.'

Now you're thrashing: An oldie but a goodie. Its name comes from the thrashing machine that used to be the centrepiece of a country harvest (and every mother's nightmare if the little ones got too near).

A real goer: If you need someone to do a few odd jobs around the house, this is the type of person you should hire. They work non-stop and drink their tea standing.

Sucking diesel: When you are really starting to get going having spent the first two hours trying to get the shagging generator to work, as in 'that's it, now we're sucking diesel!'

Going ninety to the dozen: 'I'm going ninety to the dozen' is not a bad thing to hear from a person picking potatoes, but not what you want to hear from your consultant ophthalmologist.

Giving it shit: More commonly observed towards the end of the day when light is beginning to run out, as in 'look, let's give it shit for the next hour and then finish up'.

Up to my ears: This is someone who is working almost the whole week having taken on a couple of **nixers*** to help pay for the wedding (when we say wedding, what we actually mean is the photographer he didn't want).

*nixers: Extra job taken on, which is cash in hand, done on a Saturday and something the tax man knows nothing about (yet).

Up to my eyeballs: If you hear someone tell you they are up to their eyeballs working then don't disturb them. Those 15 minutes you spend chatting to them were what they were going to use for their toilet break later.

Up to ninety: This is just the right side of too much work. When you're up to ninety you won't see the day go. If you meet someone in this state, however, it is not wise to give them another caseload of work unless you want to hear a creative place where you can stick it.

Flat out: What the week before you go on your annual holidays is like.

Like a blue-arsed fly: Imagine someone working behind a bar 15 minutes to midnight on New Year's Eve. And then imagine that the person who was helping them out has called in sick, the Guinness tap needs changing, the customers are three deep and they've run out of pint glasses. This is someone working like a blue-arsed fly.

Working your bollix off: How you describe it when you have been going all day, gotten no thanks and haven't even been given a cup of tea and a Snack bar.

NON-WORK ETHIC

Of course, there are times when we Irish are unable, unwilling or unenthusiastic when it comes to work and we have a number of words related to that too!

- **Fluting around:** The art of appearing busy but getting absolutely no work done whatsoever. Mothers are great at spotting someone who is just fluting around.

- **Diddly squat:** The actual amount of work achieved by someone who has spent the whole day fluting around.

- **Foostering:** While 'foostering' usually means hanging around or wasting time, 'fooster' can also mean kick, which is exactly what someone who 'is foostering about' could do with up their backside.

- **Chancer:** A person who on first impression appears to be working but in fact is doing little or no work.

- **Dosser:** Usually a really lazy student, particularly one who thinks that this time next year he or she will be

skulling pints at the college bar in UCD but will in fact be queue-barging for vegetable soup in their school canteen as they repeat their Leaving Cert. While dossers tend to be young in age the odd one can be found hanging around the public sector well into their 50s.

- **Clot:** A clot is not only lazy, he or she is also messy to boot. You should have rang their references.

- **Drawing the dole:** The non-art-related practice of receiving money from social welfare.

- **Signing on:** What you do when you begin drawing the dole.

- **On the scratcher:** The custom of drawing the dole.

- **Sickie:** This is when you call in sick either because you have a dose or because of a woman's issue (not a good excuse if you are a man). Sickies are most common the morning after the county final, for Friday weddings or because you worked your bollix off yesterday and they didn't even say thanks.

WORK DONE WELL

If you are ever looking for help, it is important you get someone who knows what they are doing, who's capable, who's competent, who's accomplished, who's skilled and can do the job well. Sometimes the best way to find someone like that is to ask around and listen out for the following descriptions.

A DAB HAND: A phrase that might be used for someone who's not usually associated with DIY but who is skilled and 'a dab hand' at it nonetheless.

TASTY: While the bored housewife might jump at the chance of hiring a 'tasty' tradesman, unfortunately, this says less about the face and figure and more about how neat and tidy they leave everything.

WORK NOT DONE WELL

And then it is important that you don't get someone who can't do the job properly. Be on the look-out for the following descriptions.

HALF-ARSED: This is the type of job that was started well only for the person to lose interest. Better not to be done at all than to be done 'half-arsed'.

ROUGH AS F***: You can guess the ending. Someone whose work is 'rough as' generally has no pride in their work and doesn't care if their plastering is so bad you don't know if you should look at it or climb up it.

DESCRIBING BREAKDOWNS

When done badly, it is not surprising that things inevitably break down. Never fear, however, because even if it takes a while to fix at least we have several words to describe it while it lies in pieces.

Bockety: Not broken yet but with its wobbly legs it won't take much more punishment.

Knackered: This signifies that the item has passed its sell-by-date and is well and truly worn to bits.

Banjaxed: If this wasn't broken to begin with it is now after some eejit tried to fix it and only went and made it worse.

Bollixed: This wasn't the eejit's fault. It was never going to be repaired.

Hanlin': 'Trouble'. If you heard up north that someone was having 'wile hanlin'' with their car, there is a fair to middling chance they'll not pass the NCT.

Fecked: While there is a slim chance that with either some TLC or a strong kick this might be fixable, the reality is it will need replacing in the near future.

F*cked: Don't even bother ringing MacGyver, there is absolutely no chance it'll be fixed. You'll have to replace it now.

FEELiNG FULL OF ENERGY

We have a multitude of terms for when we have lots of energy.

— **In top form:** Life is good. Your new relationship is working out. The car is running smoothly. Nailed that promotion. The team won at the weekend. Yes? Then 'life is good'.

— **In great form:** Using 'in great form' suggests that up until a week previously life wasn't the best, you were unhappily single, the fan belt needed replacing, the boss was giving you grief, the children weren't sleeping and your team couldn't buy a victory. However, due to an unexpected turn of events or how things straighten themselves out, life has turned upwards and you are now in 'great form'.

- **In flying form:** While this is without doubt the best possible form to be in, it is also a dangerous one as it can be often heard at removals – 'When I met him last week, he was in flying form! I can't believe he just upped and died!'

- **Buzzin':** While occasionally substance related, 'buzzin'' widely means to be feeling great as a result of an unexpected surprise or an occasion that has gone far better than expected.

FEELiNG NOT SO FULL OF ENERGY

Of course, for as many words and phrases we have for feeling full of energy we have an equal number for when we are not.

- **Bate/bet:** Hearing someone say 'I'm bate' or 'I'm pure bet' means that they are absolutely exhausted, usually because of a hard day's work.

- **Knackered:** Being 'knackered' or 'completely knackered' indicates probably the most common form of physical exhaustion experienced in Ireland.

- **Head's gone:** 'The head's gone' refers to mental exhaustion because you've been working on some subject matter that needed incredible attention to detail, like doing your taxes, correcting exams or trying to figure out at what angle you need to cut a piece of timber for it to fit.

- **Back is broken:** This can be for either good or bad reasons. If your own 'back is broken' then you may as well call it a day. While it does not mean that you are going to have to spend the next two weeks in a hospital bed in traction, if you don't stop now you soon will. The more positive interpretation is when you have the 'back broken' of the job, meaning it's nearly there and you can almost smell lunch.

- **Dying a death:** While this term can be used for when things are petering away towards a terrible ending, like Season 6 of *Lost*, if someone is using this about themselves it generally means they are in poor shape and cannot wait till the day is over. They are either home in front of the television or in bed asleep, and thankfully this has nothing to do with death.

- **Dying a slow death:** Same as above, but the key element of boredom is added.

TAKiNG iT EASY

It is important to look after yourself when you are not full of energy, or certainly need to recharge the batteries. There are several forms of rest that can do this for you.

- **Chill out:** When you just sit and relax.

- **Pan out:** You don't necessarily have to fall asleep for this one but you do need to make sure you are horizontal and your arms and legs are spread far and wide.

- **Forty winks:** You'll be ready to go again soon, you just need half an hour.

- **Resting your eyes:** What your Dad says to you when he doesn't want to admit to being asleep even when he needed a nap anyway. 'I was not sleeping, I was just resting my eyes.'

- **Out for the count:** Being 'out for the count' is the type of condition you are in when you finally get some sleep at the end of a stag weekend or after a double shift.

- **Kip:** 'To have a kip' is any type of unconsciousness that involves a couch.

BODY AND MIND

—

In the modern age, we need to think of our body and mind and all that goes with it.

IRISH ANATOMY

If you come across an accident where someone is being slightly unresponsive and complaining of the pain,* it may prove helpful to understand that there are parts of the body that Irish people don't always refer to as you might expect. See this helpful diagram for more.

*A word of warning, if you have come across the accident in late morning and the injured person is lying in a ditch wearing only one shoe with signs of a half-eaten snack box nearby, then in all probability they have not been in an accident but are merely hungover. At most, put a blanket over them and whoosh the cattle away.

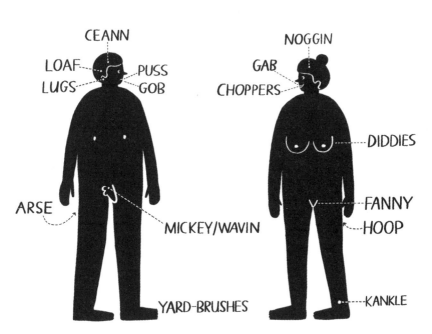

CLOTHING

Hand in hand with the Irish body are the items of clothing used to cover it. Along with the usual array of words we use for items of clothing such as T-shirts, coats, stilettos and trousers we do have a few that are distinctly our own.

JUMPER: One of the strangest-sounding items of Irish clothing, the jumper is a sweater or jersey that has absolutely nothing to do with jumping.

TOP: Commonly a jumper, the top is an item of clothing that goes above the waistline and is what Irish mothers are continually trying to get their children to put on their way out the door.

GEANSAÍ: Irish word commonly used in conversation for jumper.

TROUSERS: A term that is as popular as the more international pants.

HATS, SCARVES AND HEADBANDS: While this trio of accessories is pretty self-explanatory, it is important to note that they can only genuinely be purchased out of prams or beside lamp posts on Championship Sundays.

KAXX: Male underwear.

BRÓG: Irish for shoes, occasionally used.

KNICKERS: Any of the wide variety of female underwear.

BOBBIN: What you put in your hair to keep it in order, and despite having 143 of them lying around the house, these are impossible to find when you're in a hurry.

GÚNA: Another Irish word occasionally used for a dress, particularly one that is as shapely as a curtain.

RUNNERS: In other parts of the world they call these 'sneakers' or 'trainers'. However, for us growing up they were 'runners' because you can run in them, duh!

CLOD-HOPPERS: Shoes, particularly those big ones that would often catch you during kick-abouts.

TACKIES: Tackies are basically sneakers, or to be more specific, those rubber-soled canvas shoes. Tackies are found in only two places in the world: South Africa, where the word originated, and er ... Limerick, where the word washed up and has been used by secondary-school students for more than two generations. How it came to be in Limerick no one can be sure, but there is a story that says that a Limerick missionary came home from South Africa and brought with him the word 'tackies', which spread.

FLIP-FLOPS:
Though this might sound like a pair of populist politicians changing their minds to suit their situation, to us Irish this is a pair of sandals. A must for any would-be Irish immigrant heading Down Under and about as useful in Ireland as tits on a bull.

BUFFERS:
Nice set of trainers seen out west that weren't bought in Penneys.

HEALTH

With the advent of *Operation Transformation*, kettle bells and Zumba classes adding to Ireland's existing love of the outdoors, the health of the nation has never been better. That said, people still get sick. And while the Irish medical profession falls into line with international norms in the diagnosis of ailments, Irish people are left wanting when it comes to naming them as well.

Banger: The type of heart attack you get in Dublin, which is the same type of heart attack you get outside of Dublin, but better.

Dose: Don't worry if your Irish boyfriend rings you up and tells you it's best not to call over because he has a bit of a dose. It's not the clap, but generally some flu-like ailment he caught on the Luas. A 'dose' is a catch-all term that refers to anything from Spanish influenza to a runny nose and is the nation's favourite illness. You'll know to be on the lookout when you hear someone tell you that 'there's a bad dose doing the rounds'.

The nerves: Before we realised that it was okay to talk about mental health, we refused to even mention the 'D' word. So instead of saying 'depressed' we said that such-and-such suffered from the nerves. And with this, no further questions were asked as to why they hadn't been seen down the local lately, or asked of them when they returned to their favourite bar stool as if nothing had happened a month later.

Feeling a little down (a little low): Could mean they struggled to get out of bed due to the nerves (see above) or that they still had a bit of a dose (see above the above).

Under the weather: Could be that they were feeling down, that they were suffering from the nerves, had a bit of a dose or all of the above.

Bandy leg: This is a particularly type of mysterious chronic leg ailment that causes your leg to get sore when you're standing for long periods. Sadly, bandy-leggedness is a hereditary illness.

Scutters and trots: Not a badly-named barbershop quartet, but something a little more intestinal. While it can vary from place to place, the main difference between these two is that 'the scutters' is usually self-inflicted due to the quantity of pints consumed the previous evening. On the other hand 'the trots' is down to that dodgy chicken burger you ate on the way home.

Shook: This is more of a description than an actual ailment and is usually used for the appearance of someone who is ill. 'Shook' can mean many things from looking like you have a really bad dose of the flu to being at death's door. As result it is best not to open with this term when describing your visit to your uncle, but instead note their general malady first. Otherwise you'll have every aunt worth her salt reaching for the mass cards.

A turn: Though it sounds like someone visiting from Dublin who has gone the wrong way, to 'take a turn' is either to suddenly fall ill or to be ill and to have gotten even 'iller'.

Give up the ghost: To die. This is the final stop when the person who was 'shook' got a little better and then had 'had a turn' before finally 'giving up the ghost' and dying.

SHOCK AND SURPRISE

A common form of stress is that which comes from unwelcome shocks and surprises. Of course, not all shocks and surprises are unwelcome. I mean, just think of the National Lottery, your son surprising you by flying home from Oz or a fifth pregnancy! In Ireland we have many words that you can use for any form of shock or surprise, dominated by the Holy Family, of course.

★ **Jesus Christ!:** In fairness to the big man, he covers a lot, from the passing of a loved one to seeing your dog trying to mount your neighbour's leg.

★ **Jaysus Christ!:** Same as above, but generally used west of the Shannon.

★ **Jesus, Mary and Joseph!:** You've just won the first prize of the Toyota Corolla in the GAA raffle.

★ **Dear Jesus!:** You come home to see your three-year old has climbed up on top of the press and is sitting there laughing at you!

★ **Christ Almighty!:** It was your wife who found your three-year-old atop the press and is telling you over the phone.

★ **Janey mac!:** Little known first cousin to Jesus, this is good to use for amazement at something positive, like getting a birthday card with a tenner in it or whenever you see the happy animal story at the end of the news bulletin (like the one with the squirrel water-skiing in Australia).

★ **Bejaysus!:** When you are kind of ready for the surprise but it still gets you on the hop. Kind of like when you're half-expecting a surprise birthday party but just aren't sure. Not as commonly used as Chandler from *Friends* would have you think.

★ **Holy sh*t!:** Not good. Your reaction when you realise that you left the car window down and it's lashing.

★ **Oh my God!:** What you say in shock after having just been proposed to (even though you picked out the ring last weekend and why else would he be so keen on going up the Eiffel Tower and it closing?).

★ **God Almighty!:** For situations that are not great but could be a lot worse. Especially those that leave you exasperated like when your son gets suspended for defacing a table, Ireland go a goal down in the first 15 minutes or the internet connection goes halfway through your daily Netflix.

★ **Holy Mary Mother of God!:** A mainstay for the older generation, especially great-grandmothers. This is perfect for those surprises that just keep on giving, like when your grandchildren from Australia come home and then you realise they have also brought their children, hence the Mother of God bit at the end.

And if you are a little Holy Family-ied out, there are a couple of non-practising members of the Irish surprise family.

★ **Ah balls!:** Not a disaster, but not how you want to begin your day either. Perfect for realising you have no milk in the morning, your phone battery is dead or you forgot you were due to collect your eldest from football training ... an hour ago!

★ **F*ck me!:** Also not good, but worse than holy sh*t. This one is perfect for both surprise and continuing shock as you first see your face on television and then wonder why on earth they're showing your ugly mug on *Crimeline*!

DISBELIEF

Similar to but different from shock and surprise. When met with information Irish people can't believe, don't believe or just don't want to believe they will often respond with the following.

You're not serious?!: When you find out your friend is pregnant.

You're kidding me?!: When you find out who the father is.

You're having me on?!: When you find out where they got pregnant.

Go way, will ya: For when you realise that your friend is only pulling your leg and her husband, and not yer man from the shop, is in fact the father after all.

As if?!: A good catch-all term for hearing something unbelievable. 'Mark gave up the drink?', 'Deirdre won a holiday to Florida on the radio?', 'Jason asked her to marry him?', 'Sandra has decided to become a nun?' – as if?!

Mar ya (mar dhea): More commonly used by the older generation for 'as if'. In recent times, it has been a common response to technological advances of the 21st century. 'Mar ya you were talking to John this morning and him down in Australia!' or 'Mar dhea you paid my television licence by using that computer thing!'

Yeah, right: Very similar to 'as if' but doubles up as a response used when you want to say no and express surprise at the same time. For instance, if someone who owes you 20 quid asks you for a pint, you could say 'yeah, right', which means, 'no way am I going to buy you a pint and you owing me €20!'

Stop the lights!: Old favourite that came from an Irish quiz show that no one under 40 has ever seen called *Quicksilver*. While 'stop the lights' actually referred to the host Bunny Carr calling for the numbered lights to stop, it came to be used to express surprise, like when you saw someone beautiful, won at bingo or when someone under 40 realises that they opened *Quicksilver* by playing for just 10p!

I've never seen the likes of it: This is the surprise reserved for incidents that you may have only ever seen on the YouTube but never came across in real life until this moment.

I've never seen the bate of it!: This is just like the above except it usually refers to an event that is a little more negative than the 'likes of it'. You can also have 'never seen the bate of him', which generally refers to the actions of a male teenager, quite often your son, whose carry-on is driving you round the bend.

And then there are four favourites from Dublin.

Go on outta dat: The 'yeah right' of Dublin, which translates into the country as 'would you go away out of that'.

Me hoop: A friendly way to express disbelief around something positive. Like if you were told yer man over there at the bar fancies you, then you could reply, 'me hoop, he does.'

Me hole: Kind of like 'me hoop' except derogatory and better used when yer man you don't fancy comes over with a really cheesy chat-up line expecting to score you, 'me hole, you will!'

I will in me hole: For when someone asks you to do a ridiculous favour. See **'yeah, right'**.

CONFUSED

If ever given two spades and asked to take your pick, it can be easy to get confused. Don't worry, even if you don't have the solution, the following phrases might help you at least to describe this bewilderment.

NOT KNOWING YOUR ARSE FROM YOUR ELBOW: Where on earth do you even start?! This is like your first day on the job in a sector you didn't even know existed last week.

FLUMMOXED: When you've tried every which way you can think of and you still can't get the shagging thing to work.

FRAZZLED: Blame the kids for this one. Often results in the parent wearing at least one item of clothing inside-out.

FLOOSTERED: The state of confusion when your guests are due to arrive in 10 minutes, the fire alarm is going off and you suddenly realise you forgot to buy garlic bread/beer/cream/plates/etc.

ACTING CRAZY

For a variety of reasons, people sometime act a little crazy. In Ireland this can come in a number of forms.

- **Pure cracked:** What secondary school teachers can become when they finally hear 'I left it at home', 'the printer has no ink', 'it's done but just in the locker', 'can I show it to you tomorrow', 'I wasn't talking' too many times.

- **Doolally:** 'To go doolally' supposedly comes from the heat-related madness that was thought to come from a British transit camp in India of a similar name (Deolali). In Ireland, however, to be a bit doolally has nothing to do with heat but generally describes those half-mad half-geniuses who go around town in sandals, occasionally stopping to scribble something on a piece of paper. You will know those who are a little doolally in pubs by their dogs sitting beside them drinking a Guinness out of a bowl.

- **For the birds:** May as well be related to the person who's a little doolally except what they write on pieces of paper is not genius but gibberish.

WORRiED

While the hangover state of 'the Fear' is one of the most celebrated forms of worry and concern in Ireland, there are many more ways people seem to get upset and agitated.

Shittin' it: This nervousness usually comes from the unknowing that goes with operations, dental appointments and meeting the in-laws for the first time.

Brickin' it: This more euphemistic description of the action above is a form of worry that surrounds every type of exam from the driving test to the Leaving Cert.

RELAXiNG

Thankfully, people have become more aware of the importance of relaxing in day-to-day life and not worrying so much. In Ireland, there is a solid tradition of phrases that encourage people to calm down and take things easy.

Stád the ball: Sometimes used in its English form as 'stall the ball', this phrase started life in the schoolyards when a kick-about was brought to a temporary halt following someone getting a shot smashed into their neither regions. Since then, this phrase has been promoted into the adult world, proving particularly useful during stag weekends to gain everyone's attention and re-evaluate the night's plan of action.

Stall the digger: Though there is a slight chance you've just hit a gas pipeline, this is another 'relax' for old friends and construction mates.

Relax the kaxx: Uttered usually to someone who looks particularly stressed and impatient, 'relax the kaxx' attempts to talk down their stress levels and get them to just take their time.

Hang on a minute: This buys you exactly that, one minute, to try to come up with some other reason to persuade your friend to relax or stay around.

Hold your hour: More common in the country at least a generation ago, this friendly request, usually spoken in a pub, was often accompanied by the production of your round of drinks.

❧ THE END ❧

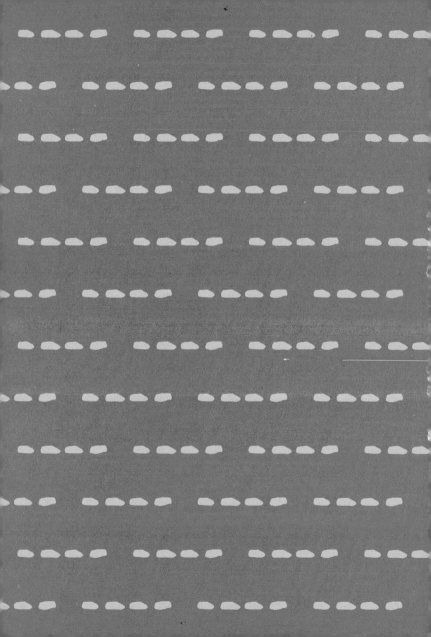